Child Abuse and Its Mimics in Skin and Bone

Child Abuse and Its Mimics in Skin and Bone

B. G. Brogdon, Tor Shwayder, Jamie Elifritz

CRC Press
Taylor & Francis Group
Boca Raton   London   New York

CRC Press is an imprint of the
Taylor & Francis Group, an **informa** business

CRC Press
Taylor & Francis Group
6000 Broken Sound Parkway NW, Suite 300
Boca Raton, FL 33487-2742

© 2013 by Taylor & Francis Group, LLC
CRC Press is an imprint of Taylor & Francis Group, an Informa business

No claim to original U.S. Government works

Printed in the United States of America on acid-free paper
Version Date: 20120709

International Standard Book Number: 978-1-4398-5535-5 (Hardback)

Library of Congress Cataloging-in-Publication Data

Brogdon, B. G. (Byron Gilliam)
    Child abuse and its mimics in skin and bone / B.G. Brogdon, Tor Shwayder, Jamie Elifritz.
      p. ; cm.
    Includes bibliographical references and index.
    ISBN 978-1-4398-5535-5 (hardback : alk. paper)
    I. Shwayder, Tor. II. Elifritz, Jamie. III. Title.
    [DNLM: 1. Child Abuse--diagnosis--Atlases. 2. Diagnosis, Differential--Atlases. 3. Forensic Medicine--methods--Atlases. 4. Skin Manifestations--Atlases. 5. Wounds and Injuries--radiography--Atlases. WA 17]

    616.85'8223--dc23
    2012026283

Visit the Taylor & Francis Web site at
http://www.taylorandfrancis.com

and the CRC Press Web site at
http://www.crcpress.com

Dedication

In memory of my precious Babs,
whose boundless love and joie de vivre
enriched my life beyond measure
and inspire me still.

B.G.B.

To the troubled parents, the children who need protection,
and the people who try to help them.

T.S.

To my parents, Barbara and Robert Elifritz,
I wish that every child could experience
the unconditional love, support, and warmth
that was ever abundant in my childhood
and continues to grow during my adult life.

J.E.

Contents

3   Radiological Mimickers of Physical Child Abuse   59

4   Dermatological Signs of Physical Abuse   141

Preface

Today it seems incredible that the intentional physical abuse of infants and children by their protectors and guardians was not recognized widely until the second half of the twentieth century. Most would agree that the publications of the radiological manifestations by John Caffey and his followers, and the intentionally inflammatory title *The Battered Child* by Henry Kempe, were the principal catalysts in the propagation of the concept.

While an expanded categorization of child abuse is recognized today—neglect, physical abuse, sexual abuse, emotional abuse—we will be concerned here almost exclusively with intentional trauma to the musculoskeletal system, soft tissues, and skin that covers them.

"Skin and bones" is a common concatenation in our everyday language, and certainly the two are closely intertwined in the diagnosis of physical abuse. Some of the musculoskeletal trauma induced is obvious from the resulting symptomatology and deformity in the victim. But, particularly in the very young, the symptoms may be unexpressed and deformation unobservable. In many instances the dermatological findings suggest the possibility and prompt the imaging studies. In others, the dermatological manifestations confirm the imaging diagnosis. In still others, the findings of either discipline can be exculpatory.

While those most likely to encounter victims of infant and child abuse—family and emergency physicians, pediatricians, nurses, social workers, educators, law enforcement personnel—have some general knowledge of the presentation of physically abused infants and children, accurate diagnosis can be difficult. This is especially true on an initial visit, which may be urgent or otherwise hurried, where accurate and complete history is absent, incomplete, or obfuscated, and laboratory studies unavailable or deferred. Under penalty of federal law and the laws of every state, the *suspicion* of child abuse must be reported to the appropriate authority. However necessary, even laudatory, the intent of this mandate, it encourages overreporting. A false accusation of child abuse can wreak multigenerational havoc in a family, sometimes unresolved for months or years, and often with long-term psychological damage. The distinction between accidental trauma and inflicted trauma may be quite vague. Nontraumatic or truly accidental conditions may simulate the lesions of abuse. Of all children reported to child protective services for suspected maltreatment in any form, the percentage of substantiated cases of physical abuse actually is quite small.

The initial suspicion of physical abuse usually comes from visual observation of the skin or radiological observation of the skeleton. But, there are a number of dermatological conditions and radiologically demonstrable musculoskeletal lesions that have been, or could be, mistaken for intentional physical abuse by the well-meaning but inexperienced or undereducated observer.

It is the purpose of this book to illustrate the classic manifestations of physical abuse by dermatological and radiological examination as a standard against which the mimickers of physical abuse can be compared. Where appropriate, pertinent historical, physical, and laboratory information in support of the correct diagnosis is included.

The authors have collected most of their examples over many years of experience in their respective fields, but acknowledge with thanks the images freely given by colleagues past and present, some as original material, others from their own publications. When possible, their generosity is acknowledged. Unfortunately, the identity of some of these benefactors is lost to record or memory in the mists of time.

Acknowledgments

Many people contribute to the production of a book, unfortunately sometimes unknowingly, unremembered, unacknowledged. They are not unappreciated, but the sands of time erode our memory and hide our records. For decades friends, colleagues, and former residents have generously provided me with images, the invaluable currency of radiological publishing. Whenever possible I have acknowledged those gifts with appropriate citation or credits. I hope those not specifically mentioned will forgive with the same spirit that prompted their initial giving.

This is the fourth book that our departmental photographer, Tolley Tollefsen, has done for me. He is a master at reproducing radiological images, improving many forensic images that are suboptimal in the original. Tolley is retiring the week I write this. It may truncate my career too; I can't imagine producing a radiological publication without him after all these years. Dr. Shwayder furnished all of the dermatological photographs, which were then sized, color/contrast adjusted, and otherwise prepped by Tolley for publication. We are indebted to Dr. Shwayder's patients for their gracious agreement to be photographed.

This is the second book Alicia Mackie, my secretary and assistant, has worked on with me. She too is masterful in translating my sometimes indecipherable cursive script into a readable manuscript. Besides that, she relieves me of the onerous administrative tasks attending the production of a book—permissions, interlibrary loans, communications with coauthors, contributors, and publishers, and the like. I hope she doesn't retire before I do!

In this and all scholarly activities, I must recognize my indebtedness to the hundreds of residents with whom I have had the privilege of "training"; from them, I always have learned much more than I have taught.

It has been a pleasure to work with Taylor & Francis/CRC Press again. Amy Blalock, senior project coordinator for this book, and Amy Rodriguez, senior project editor, have been most agreeably effective in protecting me from many of the petty annoyances frequently encountered in the production phase of a book. Finally, I acknowledge with great appreciation and affection the encouragement, support, and wise advice received from Becky McEldowney Masterman, senior acquisition editor for Taylor & Francis/CRC Press, and a treasured longtime friend.

Gil Brogdon

About the Authors

B.G. Brogdon, MD, FACR, grew up on a farm in Arkansas where he graduated from the state university and its school of medicine. He began his residency training there and completed it at Bowman Gray School of Medicine of Wake Forest University. During his 60 years in radiology he has pursued special interests in pediatric, musculoskeletal, and forensic radiology—hence this book.

His academic career has included faculty appointments at the University of Florida; as radiologist in charge, Division of Diagnostic Radiology, Johns Hopkins; chair of the Department of Radiology at the University of New Mexico; and now as University Distinguished Professor Emeritus and former chair at the University of South Alabama.

Gil Brogdon is a member of many professional organizations. Offices and honors include past president and gold medalist, American College of Radiology; past president and gold medalist of the Association of University Radiologists; past president of the Southern Radiological Conference; gold medalist of the American Roentgen Ray Society; honorary member and Schinz medalist of the Swiss Society of Medical Radiology; silver medalist of the International Skeletal Society; medal of honor, Leopold-Franzen University (Innsbrinck); Cross of Honor, First Class (Austria); and Hunt Award and Distinguished Fellow Award and Medal, American Academy of Forensic Sciences. He is patron of the International Association of Forensic Radiographers and charter/honorary member of the International Association of Forensic Radiology and Imaging.

He is the author, coauthor, or editor of some 360 publications, including the classic *Brogdon's Forensic Radiology* (CRC Press), now in its second edition, and the prize-winning *Atlas of Abuse, Torture Terrorism and Inflicted Trauma* (CRC Press).

Tor Shwayder, MD, FAAP, FAAD, is a native of Detroit. He received a BA from Harvard University and attended the University of Michigan for medical school and pediatric residency. He was in pediatric practice for a short while before attending the University of Rochester Strong Memorial Hospital for dermatology training. He has been Director of Pediatric Dermatology at Henry Ford Hospital since 1987. Dr. Shwayder is a lifelong violinist with a degree from the Royal Academy of Music in London as a violin teacher. He is also an avid private pilot and spends most weekends with his head in the clouds.

Jamie Elifritz, MD, DABR, is a graduate of the Wright State School of Medicine in Dayton, Ohio. She became immersed in forensic radiology as a radiology resident under the direction of Dr. Brogdon at the University of South Alabama in Mobile. She completed a musculoskeletal and forensic radiology fellowship at the University of New Mexico in Albuquerque, where she now occupies the position of assistant professor. She has a combined appointment in the Department of Radiology and the Department of Pathology and is a member of the Center for Forensic Imaging at the Office of the Medical Examiner for the State of New Mexico. Dr. Elifritz is a member of the American Academy of Forensic Sciences and the American College of Radiology. In her free time, she enjoys traveling as well as spending time with her family, friends, and pets. She is a lifelong soccer player and an active runner.

The Concept of Child Abuse in Historical Perspective

1

John Caffey, MD (Figure 1.1), was a pediatrician *cum* pediatric radiologist at New York City's Babies Hospital when in 1946 he published a paper entitled "Multiple Fractures in Long Bones of Children Suffering from Chronic Subdural Hematoma."[1] In that paper he candidly expressed his puzzlement at this concatenation of findings for which there was no predisposing disease or appropriate history to explain these injuries, although they appeared to be of traumatic origin. Nor was there explanation for the chronic subdural hematomas that, after years of controversy, were once again accepted as usually due to trauma.[2-6]

Caffey's paper was the catalyst that finally awakened the medical profession and the public to recognition of an evil existing for thousands of years.[3] Indeed, child abuse would have been considered an oxymoron for 98% of the span of recorded history. From ancient and biblical times the child was simply a chattel subject to the absolute power of the paternal parent or his surrogate. The child could be abused, abandoned, apprenticed, maimed, enslaved, indentured, put to death, or cut in half.[3,7,8] The child's fate was tempered only by the uncertain conscience of the parent or guardian. Harsh discipline and vicious punishment were tolerated (with approbation in many instances) by civic and religious authorities.[3] The plight of these poor children was exacerbated by the Industrial Revolution, as they were found to be cheap, efficient, and expendable in the mills.[2,3]

A few influential writers inveighed against the prevalent exploitation and maltreatment of children. The most effective of them in England and America was Charles Dickens, who as a 12-year-old had personally endured a humiliating year drudging in a blacking factory while his father was in debtor's prison.[9] Tales of cruel treatment gradually elicited a societal response in the United States. The Society for the Prevention of Cruelty to Children was established in 1871 under the umbrella of the Society for the Prevention of Cruelty to Animals, after successful arguments that children were members of the animal kingdom. A similar organization was established in England 18 years later.[1,4]

Prior to the mid-twentieth century, the medical profession seems to have been mostly oblivious to, or unconcerned with, the possibility of inflicted injuries to infants and children. Sadly, an explicit and detailed description of child abuse was published in 1860.[10] Ambroise Tardieu (1818–1879) was a French physician specializing in pathology, public health, and legal medicine, as well as being professor of the latter discipline at the University of Paris (Figure 1.2). His germinal paper[10] (Figure 1.3), republished in his 1879 book[11] (Figure 1.4), described every aspect of inflicted childhood trauma except the radiological. He described the typical injuries, the demographics of the victims and perpetrators, the emotional response of the abused, and he clearly identified caregivers as the victimizers. Unfortunately, Tardieu's work apparently had little impact on his contemporaries and the essential elements of the syndrome awaited rediscovery almost nine decades later.

1

Figure 1.1 John Caffey (1895–1978), the father of pediatric radiology. He first described radiological findings of child abuse in 1946. (From Girdany, B.R., et al., *AJR Am J Roentgenol* 1979; 132:149–50. With permission.)

Figure 1.2 Ambroise Tardieu (1818–1879). He described all of the salient features of physical child abuse (except the radiological) almost 90 years before Caffey's seminal paper. (From Silverman, F.N., *Radiology* 1972; 104:337–353. With permission.)

Caffey's original description[1] of the skeletal abnormalities associated with the subdural hematomas included multiple fractures in long bones with unusual metaphysical fragmentation and large "involucrums" (because they resembled the findings of chronic osteomyelitis, a common disease of that time). He also noted a pattern of fractures in different stages of healing. He could not explain a "causal mechanism" for this peculiar combination of findings.

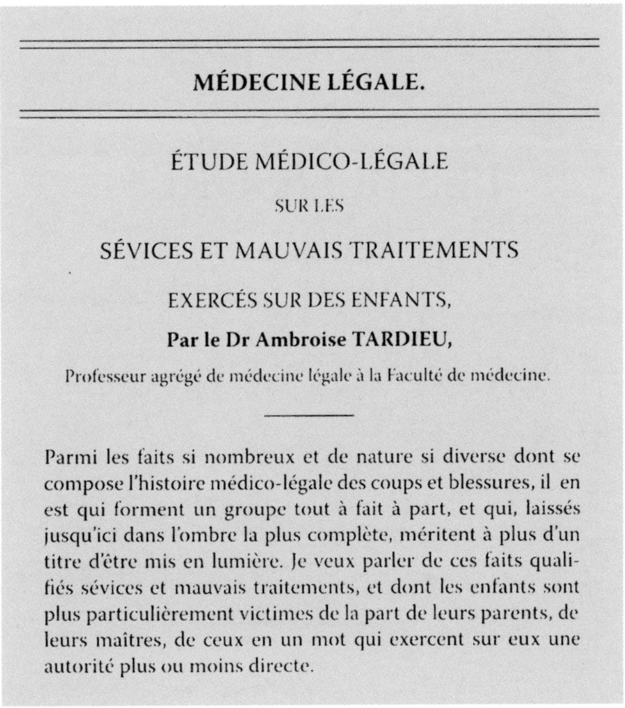

MÉDECINE LÉGALE.

ÉTUDE MÉDICO-LÉGALE

SUR LES

SÉVICES ET MAUVAIS TRAITEMENTS

EXERCÉS SUR DES ENFANTS,

Par le Dr Ambroise TARDIEU,

Professeur agrégé de médecine légale à la Faculté de médecine.

Parmi les faits si nombreux et de nature si diverse dont se compose l'histoire médico-légale des coups et blessures, il en est qui forment un groupe tout à fait à part, et qui, laissés jusqu'ici dans l'ombre la plus complète, méritent à plus d'un titre d'être mis en lumière. Je veux parler de ces faits qualifiés sévices et mauvais traitements, et dont les enfants sont plus particulièrement victimes de la part de leurs parents, de leurs maîtres, de ceux en un mot qui exercent sur eux une autorité plus ou moins directe.

Figure 1.3 First page of Tardieu's 1860 paper on child abuse. (From Silverman, F.N., *Radiology* 1972; 104:337–353. With permission.)

As the Mackenzie Davidson Memorial lecturer in 1957,[12] Caffey added some new radiographic features: traumatic bowing of the ends of diaphyses secondary to metaphyseal infractions, metaphysical "cupping," and "ectopic ossification centers."

In yet another communication in 1965,[13] Caffey discussed the relative values of the history, physical examination, laboratory findings, biopsy results, and radiographic manifestations in the diagnostic process of this condition. He noted that the history of trauma was often withheld. Still cautious and uncondemning, he suggested that the history of trauma was sometimes unknown to the family. He maintained that although "the radiographic changes are pathognomonic of trauma … they never identify the perpetrator … or his motive." Caffey still believed that "the great majority of simple, even serious, traumatic episodes in children … are accidents for which no one is responsible."

The reluctance to lay blame, and the continual benefit of doubt regarding the victimizers of these nonvocal children, is incredible to us today. Careful disclaimers excluded a catalog of intercurrent conditions—infection, malnutrition, avitaminosis, metabolic bone disease—as contributory factors. Euphemistic names for the syndrome suggested a mysterious etiology of the trauma: hidden, concealed, denied, unsuspected, clandestine, etc. Caffey himself suggested *parent-infant trauma stress syndrome* (PITS).[14] *Parental dysfunction* was offered to avoid antiparental bias and suggests parental self-control is paralyzed by psychoemotional storms.[15]

Disciples of Caffey in Cincinnati (Figure 1.5) and Pittsburgh further studied the problem, and Silverman's landmark paper of 1953[16] finally focused attention on the entity and caretakers as the causative factor, whether by intention or neglect of safety.[17] Bert

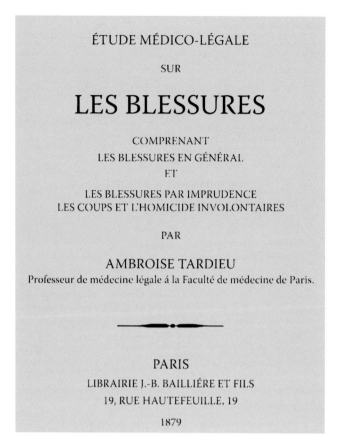

Figure 1.4 Title page of Tardieu's posthumous 1879 book on wounds included a reprinting of his 1860 article on child abuse. (From Silverman, F.N., *Radiology* 1972; 104:337–353. With permission.)

Girdany (Figure 1.6) in Pittsburgh organized a team consisting of a pediatrician, a pediatric psychiatrist, a pediatric radiologist, and a social worker. The success of this team approach was reported in Elizabeth Elmer's influential book, *Children in Jeopardy*, in 1967.[18]

A distinguished pediatrician, Henry Kempe (Figure 1.7) shocked the nation into awareness of the problem of child abuse with an intentionally inflammatory title, "The Battered Child Syndrome." The article was published in the *Journal of the American Medical Association*,[19] which at that time was probably the most widely circulated medical journal in America—if not the world.

Most of the earlier papers on physical abuse were in the radiological literature. Certainly, the concept of child abuse is that discipline's finest contribution to the forensic sciences. But the radiologists' encounters with child abuse were often in the course of examination of the infant or child for other clinical diagnoses or for other indications. The adjective "unsuspected" appeared before abuse or injury in many instances of early descriptions. Obviously, the first opportunities for suspicion or diagnosis of inflicted trauma fall to the first responders—pediatricians, family physicians, emergency physicians, social workers, school nurses, and other child care professionals.

On December 18, 1962, the American College of Radiology produced a Medical X-Ray Forum for Science Writers in New York City: "Unsuspected Trauma in Children: The Battered

Figure 1.5 Frederick N. Silverman (1914–2006), a former student and associate of Caffey. He made significant early contributions to the study of child abuse while director of the Division of Radiology at Cincinnati Children's Hospital, a post he held for 25 years. (Courtesy Lane Donnely, MD, and the Department of Radiology at Cincinnati Children's Hospital.)

Figure 1.6 Bertram Girdany, while Chief of Pediatric Radiology at Children's Hospital of Pittsburgh, organized a team approach to the problem of nonaccidental trauma to infants and children. Dr. Caffey graced Girdany's department after retiring from Babies Hospital until his death in 1978.

Child Syndrome." Pediatric radiologist Fred Silverman, Elizabeth Elmer (who wrote *Children in Jeopardy*), and an attorney, William F. Martin, introduced the concept to the premier scientific writers for popular newspapers and magazines for the general public. It was the first public notice of this special legal and medical condition, and it was widely covered in the national press.[20]

Figure 1.7 Henry Kempe (1922–1984) coined the term *battered child* while professor and chair, Department of Pediatrics at University of Colorado, after conducting the first symposium on that subject at the American Academy of Pediatrics. (From American Medical Association, *Arch Pediatr Adolescent Med* 1984; 138(3):222–3. All rights reserved.)

The American Academy of Pediatrics conducted a symposium on the problem of child abuse, under the guidance of Henry Kempe, in 1961.[3] This was followed by the landmark multidisciplinary paper by Kempe et al., which received widespread distribution via the enormous circulation of the *Journal of the American Medical Association.*[19]

The College of American Pathology devoted a half day of its 1976 annual meeting to an in-depth program on child abuse featuring a pathologist, a radiologist, a pediatrician, and a jurist.[21–25]

Papers on the intentional trauma of infants and children appearing on the programs and in the journals of the other primary case specialists and general physicians recognized that the first possibility for prospective diagnosis or suspicion of child abuse resided within their ranks.[26–28]

Trauma—Inflicted or Accidental?

The skin is the largest organ of the human body in terms of surface area exposed to the insults of ordinary living from infancy to old age. As T. Tjin-A-Tsoi so aptly puts it, "Childhood is a playful journey of discovery with at times painful consequences."[29] Bruises, scrapes, lacerations, and burns are the badges of growth and development of the vigorous child. So too are strains, sprains, and fractures. More serious accidents are the leading cause of death among infants and children from ages 1 year through age 24.[30] Differentiating accidental injuries appropriate to the age, development, and activity of the child from inflicted trauma is a serious and often difficult diagnostic challenge.

A symbiotic relationship exists between the dermatological and radiological examinations in the successful detection and diagnosis of inflicted trauma to infants and children.

Suspicious skin lesions may indicate skeletal survey. Radiological referral for a focal indication may suggest visual inspection of the entire body, including retinae and genitalia. The benefits of a combined approach exceed those of the individual disciplines. The purpose of this book is to emphasize that combination in either the diagnosis or exclusion of inflicted trauma to an infant or child, either possibility being of infinite importance to both the child and his or her caretaker(s).

Incidence of Inflicted Trauma

It must be admitted that the true incidence of physical abuse of infants and children is unknown, and probably unknowable on a global basis. Increasing numbers of cases of child abuse and neglect are reported annually. This probably reflects improved recognition and reportage by community professionals.[26] The relative incidence of abuse has diminished as reported neglect has increased.[31] Many cases are unrecognized and unreported. There are inevitable statistical disagreements in the literature for lack of standardization.

There is not even a standard definition of abuse in the United States, although every state has mandatory reporting laws. Some condone certain levels of corporal punishment by parents and teachers; others do not.[32] Local standards of responsibility for child safety are inconsistent. Abuse, per se, does not rest on definition as much as on conceptualization. The concept is inextricably entangled in historical, religious, and cultural considerations. Thus the definition of abuse is widely variable within geographical boundaries, over the passage of time, and with the evolution of religious and societal mores.[33] Regardless of imprecise numbers and inconsistent statistics, intentional physical traumatization of infants and children is a problem of global importance, both medically and socially.

The figure of 3 million cases per year is mentioned for "child abuse,"[31] or for "maltreatment,"[34] or for "abuse and neglect,"[26] nicely illustrating the imprecision of reporting what is presumably the same data. Neglect is at least two to three times as common as physical abuse.[30,31] Up to 1,200 deaths per year from physical trauma can be expected from this group.[30] The most common cause of fatality is head trauma; however, a remarkable 20% of abusive deaths by gunshot in a U.S. Air Force study[35] demonstrates cultural variability.

The incidence of abuse diminishes with the increasing age of the child. Infants (less than 1 year old) account for almost half of abuse-related fatalities.[30] The incidence of fractures from physical abuse ranges from 11 to 55% in the literature. The difference is related to the age of children in the groups studied,[36] and about half are found in infants less than 1 year old. The incidence rises to as much as 94% in children 3 and under. Although hematomas, contusions, and bruises are the most prevalent injuries in inflicted trauma, fractures may be the first sign of abuse in as many as one in five children.[37-39]

Risk Factors

Although, as always, a few "outlier" opinions can be found, there is a workable consensus for risk factors for inflicted physical trauma to infants and children:[4,19,28,31,32,34,40]

1. *The victim*: Product of an unwanted pregnancy, prematurity, low birth weight, congenital or developmental handicap, chronic illness or just "sickly" (cries a lot), disappointing performer or achiever, female rather than male gender.

2. *Parental*: Previously abused parent, spousal abuse, immature parenting skill—age related or psychological, depression, single-parent family, unwilling caretaker (family or nonfamily), substance abuse, unreasonable expectations of the child, misguided confidence in partner—marital or nonmarital.
3. *Socioeconomic*: Poverty, underrepresented minority, violent society (more common in United States than in 17 other developed countries; 75% of violence in the United States is domestic violence), cultural and religious practices.
4. *Perpetrators*: Family—husbands, then boyfriends, then mothers, then foster parents and institutions, in declining percentages.

Suspicion, Substantiation, or Exclusion of Inflicted Trauma

The suspicion of intentionally inflicted trauma may derive from a serendipitous observation on a radiological examination requested for an entirely different clinical indication. That suspicion then may prompt a more thorough physical re-examination of the patient and the historical antecedents leading to the imaging referral.

On the other hand, the initial examination, history, and physical findings may prompt referral for an extensive radiological survey.

Dermatologic Survey

The complete dermatological survey and documentation of a suspected case of physical child abuse should include:

1. Recording of vital signs
2. Inspection of all body surfaces for bruises, welts, swelling, scrapes or abrasions, lacerations, scars, burns, bite marks, tourniquet or ligature impressions, patchy hair loss
3. Palpation of all reachable bony structures
4. Genital inspection
5. Checking of eyes for sclera or retinal abnormalities; nose for deformity, blood; ears for bruising of pinna or in postauricular soft tissue; mouth, externally for lip swelling, cuts, palpebral corner tears or fissures, and internally for cuts, bruises, traumatized teeth, torn frenubum
6. Documentation in writing or by diagram of all abnormalities describing size and configuration or, ideally, color photography with a measuring device in the field of view

Radiologic Survey

Radiologically, the "babygram"—the radiography of all or most of an infant or small child with a single exposure—is not an acceptable survey technique.[28] It is true that a suspicious finding may be appreciated on such an image. But a dependable survey of the infant or young child for physical abuse demands good technique, and careful positioning of the patient to acquire several individual films or digital exposures to cover

Table 1.1 The Routine Skeletal Survey

Frontal and lateral skull

AP supine and lateral chest (including visualization of the lateral thoracic spine)

AP lumbar spine and pelvis

Lateral lumbar spine

AP upper extremities[a] (with forearms in supination)

PA hands

AP lower extremities[a] (with toes slightly inverted)

AP feet

[a] Beyond infancy expose arms and forearms, thighs and legs separately for more uniform density and better detail.

the entire body.[4,41–43]A complete radiological skeletal survey must include the following (Table 1.1): two views of the skull, entire spine, chest and abdomen, as well as all four extremities, including the hands and feet. Skull films are essential even when a CT of the head is done because linear fractures of the skull may be missed if parallel to the axial plane or "slice" of the CT images. Unless imaged separately, hands and feet will not be properly positioned or exposed. Past infancy, extremities should be imaged in two parts rather than as a continuum. This routine may require as many as 12–17 individual film or digital images, depending on the size and development of the child. Beyond age 5, the ability of the child to demonstrate or vocalize his or her problem, in consonance with the history and physical findings, may allow more localized concentration of the initial radiological examination. However, ruling out all injuries will again require the entire survey.

Any evidence of head injury or visceral injury will require additional, usually sectional imaging, procedures (i.e., CT, MRI, nuclear imaging, ultrasonography), but this is beyond the purview of this book.

The same standard should apply to postmortem radiographic surveys to determine the cause and manner of death in cases of sudden infant death syndrome (SIDS), unexplained death in infancy, or to catalog the extent of injuries in cases of inflicted trauma. However, a recent survey[44] of 259 pathologists who perform autopsies on children revealed that nearly one-third of them only obtain one or two images (babygram). Only 5% obtain the full survey. Budgetary constraints were the common explanation for this limitation.

Clinical history, physical examination, laboratory studies, and radiological examination—each can contribute to the substantiation of inflicted trauma or an exclusionary diagnosis of accidental injury or other medical conditions.[4,13,19,28,31,45]

Clinical suspicion should be aroused when any injury is inconsistent with the age, development, and activity level of the child. Similarly, a provided history that is inconsistent with the finding or that is inconsistent on repetition raises suspicion. Multiple caretakers or observers are ideally questioned singly. If the child can verbalize his or her complaint or describe the incident, questioning away from caretakers is recommended if at all possible. Many factors require consideration before a final differentiation between abuse and nonabuse can be decided with reasonable medical certainty. The correct diagnosis may save the life of a child; conversely, an erroneous diagnosis of inflicted trauma can irreparably rend the fabric of an innocent family.

References

1. Caffey, J. 1946. Multiple fractures in long bones of children suffering from chronic subdural hematoma. *AJR Am J Roentgenol* 56:163–73.
2. Silverman, F.N. 1972. Unrecognized trauma in infants, the battered child syndrome, and the syndrome of Ambroise Tardieu: Rigler lecture. *Radiology* 104:337–53.
3. Radbill, S.X. 1974. A history of child abuse and infanticide. In Helfer, R.E., and Kempe, C.H., eds., *The battered child*, 2nd ed. University of Chicago Press, Chicago, chap. 1.
4. Hall, C. 1944. In Carty, H., Shaw, D., Brunnelle, F., and Kendall, B., eds., *Imaging children*, vol. 2. Churchill Livingston, London, 1188–89.
5. Sherwood, P. 1930. Chronic subdural hematoma in infants. *Am J Dis Child* 39:980–1021.
6. Ingraham, E.D., and Heyle, H.L. 1939. Subdural hematoma in infants and children. *JAMA* 112:198–204.
7. Brogdon, B.G. 1998. *Forensic radiology*. CRC Press, Boca Raton, FL, 281.
8. Holy Bible. King James Version. 1 Kings 3:16–28.
9. Slater, M. 2009. *Charles Dickens*. Yale Press, New Haven, CT, 20–24.
10. Tardieu, A. 1860. Étude médico-légale sur les sévices et mauvais traitements exercés sur des infants. *Ann Hyg Publ Med Leg* 13:361–98.
11. Tardieu, A. 1879. *Étude médico-légale sur les blessures*. J-B Bailliere et fils, Paris.
12. Caffey, J. 1957. Some traumatic lesions in growing bones other than fractures and dislocations, clinical and radiographic features. *Br J Radiol* 30:225.
13. Caffey, J. 1965. Significance of the history in the diagnosis of traumatic injury to children: Howland Award Address. *J Pediatr* 68:1008–14.
14. Caffey, J. 1972. The parent-infant traumatic stress syndrome (battered child syndrome). *AJR Am J Roentgenol* 114:217–29.
15. Galdston, R. 1965. Observations on children who have been physically abused and their parents. *Am J Psychiatry* 122:440–43.
16. Silverman, F. 1953. The Roentgen manifestation of unrecognized skeletal trauma in infants. *AJR Am J Roentgenol* 69:413–27.
17. Johnson, C.F. 1990. Inflicted injury versus accidental injury. *Pediatr Clin North Am* 37:791–813.
18. Elmer, E. 1967. *Children in jeopardy*. University of Pittsburgh Press, Pittsburgh, PA.
19. Kempe, C.H., Silverman, F.H., Steele, B.F., Droegemueller, W., and Silver, H.K. 1962. The battered child syndrome. *JAMA* 181:17–24.
20. Annual Report. 1976. Cooperative program in public information. Sponsored by the American College of Radiology and the Eastman Kodak Co., 8.
21. Manwaring, J.H. 1977. Child abuse and neglect: An overview. *Pathologist* 31:125–26.
22. Weston, J.T. 1997. The role of the pathologist in the investigation and examination of child abuse victims. *Pathologist* 31:127–33.
23. Brogdon, B.G. 1977. Child abuse: The radiologist's role. *Pathologist* 21:134–36.
24. Garff, R.S., Jr. 1977. Child abuse and court procedure. *Pathologist* 31:190–96.
25. Apthrop, J.S. 1977. Child abuse: The role of the pediatrician. *Pathologist* 31:197–98.
26. Jain A.M. 1999. Emergency department evaluation of child abuse. *Emer Med Clin North Am* 17:575–93.
27. Bullock, K. 2000. Child abuse: The physician's role in alleviating a growing problem. *Am Fam Physician* 61:2977–79.
28. Pressel, D.M. 2000. Evaluation of physical abuse in children. *Am Fam Physician* 61:3057–64.
29. Tjin-A-Tsoi, T. 2010. Foreword I. In Bilo, R.A.C., Robben, S.G.F., and van Rjin, R.R., *Forensic aspects of paediatric fractures*. Springer, Berlin, vii.
30. Lonergan, G.J., Baker, A.M., Morey, M.K., and Boos, S.C. 2003. Child abuse: Radiologic-pathologic correlation. *Radiographics* 23:811–45.
31. Bethea, L. 1999. Primary prevention of child abuse. *Am Fam Physician* 59:1577–85.
32. Johnson, C.F. 1999. Inflicted injury versus accidental injury. *Pediatr Clin North Am* 37:791–814.

33. Brogdon, B.G. 2010. Radiology of abuse. In Thali, M., Viner, M.D., and Brogdon, B.G., eds., *Brogdon's forensic radiology*, 2nd ed. CRC Press, Boca Raton, FL, 255–60.
34. Lane, W.G. 2003. Diagnosis and management of physical abuse in children. *Clin Fam Pract* 5:493–514.
35. Lucas, D.R., Wezner, K.C., Milner, J.S., et al. 2002. Victim, perpetrator, family, and incident characteristics of infant and child homicide in the United States Air Force. *Child Abuse Negl* 26:167–86.
36. Kleinman, P.K. 1998. *Diagnosis imaging of child abuse*, 2nd ed. Mosby, St. Louis, 8–9.
37. McMahon, P., Grossman, W., Gaffney, M., et al. 1995. Soft tissue injury as an indication of child abuse. *J Bone Jt Surg* 77:1179–83.
38. Cramer, K.E. 1996. Orthopedic aspects of child abuse. *Pediatr Clin North Am* 43:1035–51.
39. Sinai, S.H., and Stewart, C.D. 1998. Physical abuse of children: A review for orthopedic surgeons. *J South Orthop Assoc* 7:264–76.
40. Davis, H.W., and Carraseo, M.M. 2002. Child abuse and neglect. In Zitelli, B., and Davis, H.W. eds., *Atlas of pediatric physical abuse*, 4th ed. Mosby, Philadelphia, 162–3.
41. Kleinman, P.K., DiPietro, M.A., Brody, A.S., et al. 2009. Diagnostic imaging of child abuse: Policy statement from the Section on Radiology, American Academy of Pediatrics. *Pediatrics* 123:1430–35.
42. Kemp, A.M., Butler, A., Morris, S., et al. 2006. Which radiological investigations should be performed to identify fractures in suspected child abuse? *Clin Radiol* 61:723–36.
43. American College of Radiology. 2005. Expert Panel on Pediatric Imaging. American College of Radiology: ACR Appropriateness Criteria. Suspected physical abuse—child. In *ACR Appropriateness Criteria*. American College of Radiology, Reston, VA.
44. Laskey, A.L., Habukorn, K.L., Applegate, K.E., and Catellier, M.J. 2009. Postmortem skeletal survey practices in pediatric forensic autopsies: A national survey. *J Forens Sci* 54:189–91.
45. Bilo, R.A.C., Robben S.G.F., and van Rijn, R.R. 1999. *Forensic aspects of paediatric fractures*. Springer, Berlin, 1.

Musculoskeletal Trauma in Infants and Children: Accidental or Inflicted?

2

Part 1: Introduction

Musculoskeletal trauma is common in the healthy normal child. In the unhealthy or non-normal child, the incidence of musculoskeletal trauma may be either increased or decreased, depending on his or her malady, anomaly, or defect, the coincidental limitations of activity or development incurred, and the reaction of caretakers and contemporaries engendered by these factors. We will consider first the hazards of the normal child.

Injuries to the integument and soft tissues surrounding the skeleton are rarely disabling to any serious degree or of long-term duration; bruises, scrapes, cuts, and burns may be the harbingers of inflicted trauma of more serious import. These will be discussed in Chapter 4.

Injuries to the Bones and Joints in Children: Incidence

A longitudinal study of fractures in children conducted in Malmö, Sweden, from 1950 to 1983 showed that the chances of sustaining a fractured bone between birth and 16 years was 42% for boys and 27% for girls.[1,2] Thus the chance of sustaining a fracture per year was 2.6% for boys and 1.7% for girls. This was consistent with the incidence of 1.6%/year (boys and girls combined) for fractures treated clinically in England.[3] Only 6.8% of fractures sustained by children during the first 10 years of life require admittance to the hospital.[4] Of children brought to the hospital because of injury, slightly fewer than one in five had sustained a fracture.[4] It is likely that fracture incidence was higher in earlier centuries because of life generally being more hazardous. Children were more involved in outdoor activities, there was little if any protective gear, hazardous child labor was permitted or condoned, and child protective concerns were slim to none. These factors still may elevate injury statistics in less developed countries or societies.

Physical abuse may not result in a clinically apparent injury; however, it is estimated that 90% of physically abused children ultimately suffer overt injury. By far, the most common injuries are to the skin and subcutaneous soft tissues and rarely require hospital admission or even medical treatment. Of those children under age 5 who are brought to medical attention for injuries, only about 10% are nonaccidental. Fractures are the result of more severe physical abuse and may be the first sign in 20% of those ultimately diagnosed as nonaccidental trauma.

The Dilemma of Discrimination

If injury to the skin and skeleton is a relatively common event in the life of a child, how can one discriminate between accidental and inflicted trauma? Virtually identical skeletal injuries can be sustained from intent or accident and, to some extent, in adults as well. However, there are substantial differences between the skeletal tissues of children and adults anatomically, physiologically, and biomechanically.[5–8]

13

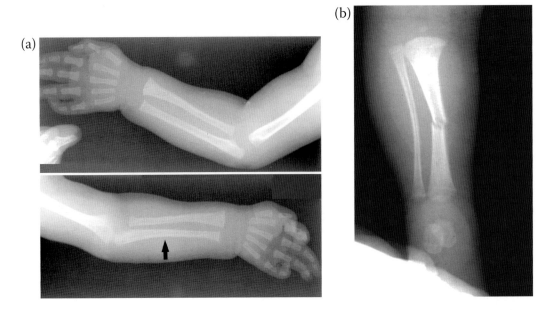

Figure 2.1 (a) Upper, normal forearm. Lower, bowing, or plastic fracture of the ulna (arrow) showing no disruption of the cortex, normal radius. (b) Transverse angulated fracture of the tibia with associated bowing fracture of the fibula. (From Rich, J., *Forensic Medicine of the Lower Extremity*, Humana Press, Totowa, NJ, 2005, p. 178, Figure 49. With permission of Springer Science+Business Media.)

The first of these major differences is related to the larger and more extensive pattern of Haversian canals in children's bones, allowing greater elasticity and malleability. Consequently, one sees in the *diaphysis* (shaft) of long bones in children bowing fractures (Figure 2.1) or the incomplete buckle or torus fracture (Figure 2.2) or the greenstick fracture (Figure 2.3). These are not seen in the mature or adult bone. The adult or mature bony response to diaphysical stresses—transverse, oblique, spiral, or "butterfly" fractures (Figure 2.4)—may also be encountered in the child, but here the context of the cause or mechanism of injury is of paramount importance.

The second major difference between child and adult skeletal injury is centered on the growth plate or *physis* between the *metaphysis* or expanded terminal end of the *diaphysis* and the *epiphysis* (*apophysis*, in the case of a nonarticular growth center) (Figure 2.5) representing a secondary growth center. The classic metaphyseal lesion (CML) of nonaccidental trauma in infants and young children was named, defined, and described by Kleinman (the *doyen* of child abuse radiology) and Marks in a series of seminal articles in the 1990s[9–12] and resides in that area.

In the physis, the cartilaginous growth plate histologically shows a progression of developmental zones proceeding to the metaphysis from resting cartilage to proliferating cartilage to maturing cartilage to calcification of osteoid around the cartilaginous columns. The dying calcified cartilage is gradually invaded by immature trabeculae of spongy bone at the extreme growing end of the metaphysis. It is through this area of immature spongiosal bone, not the cartilaginous physis, that the growing bone is disrupted or fractured by transverse shearing forces (Figure 2.6).

The CML is virtually pathognomonic of inflicted trauma due to shearing forces horizontally directed across the immature bone at the extreme end of the metaphysis. It is

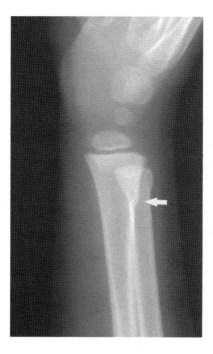

Figure 2.2 Torus or buckle fractures of the distal radius.

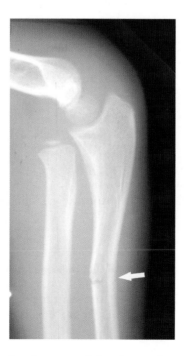

Figure 2.3 Greenstick (incomplete fracture of the ulna at the junction of the upper and middle one-thirds). Only the anterior cortex is disrupted. The posterior cortex (arrow) is intact. Normal radius.

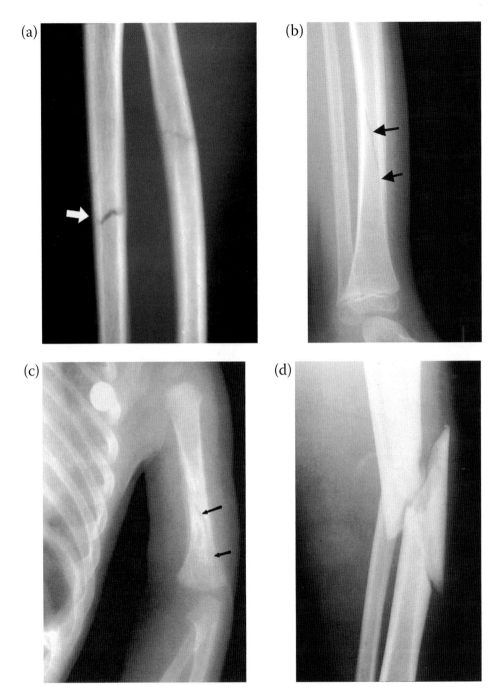

Figure 2.4 (a) Undisplaced transverse fracture of the ulna (arrow). (b) Subtle oblique fracture of the tibia (arrows). (c) Healing spiral fracture of the humerus (arrows). Notice the subperiosteal new bone surrounding and stabilizing the entire shaft of the bone. (d) Butterfly fracture of the midshaft of the tibia. The apex of the triangular or wedge-shaped fragment points away from the impact site.

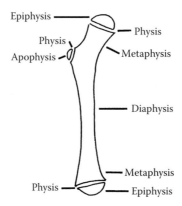

Figure 2.5 Schematic representation of a growing long bone illustrating descriptive anatomical names for the several parts or areas.

found almost exclusively in the infant or toddler in the first 18–24 months of life.[13] In the older child, once epiphyseal-diaphyseal fusion is complete, the Salter-Harris type fracture[14] is encountered (Figure 2.7). Here the principal injury appears to directly affect the physis with (in most instances) propagation of fracture lines into adjacent areas of the bony epiphysis or metaphysis. These fractures can result from either accidental or inflicted trauma.

The third major difference between fractures in children and adults depends on characteristics of the periosteum.[5] The pediatric periosteum is thicker and more biologically active than that of the adult. This results in faster healing and remodeling of fractures in infants and children than in adults. A consequence of this is that pediatric fractures are more self-stabilized by the abundant post-traumatic periosteal reaction (Figures 2.4c and 2.8).

These differences notwithstanding, the determination of whether a skeletal injury is accidental or abusive can be extremely difficult and sometimes simply impossible. The problem is exacerbated by the lack of uniformity or precision in the definition of abuse. Every jurisdiction outlawing abuse has the prerogative, usually exercised, of defining it. Thus the legal definitions can be skewed by ambiguous adjectives (i.e., substantial, unjustified, allowable), or the amount of leeway allowed in disciplining a child before the bounds of human behavior are exceeded, or by local custom, religious and cultural practices, and by the individual biases of those responsible for reporting abuse. All of these variables erode any possibility of a universal concept.[15]

Unfortunately, the law is ordinarily much clearer as to the fate of a mandated reporter of suspected abuse who fails his duty. "Unfortunately," because this encourages over-reporting as a self-defensive tactic.

Context Is Critical

Apart from the high specificity of the CML and, as discussed later, rib fractures, and the significance of the type and location of certain injuries, the decision of accidental versus nonaccidental hinges heavily on *context*. Is the injury consonant with the age, development, and activity level of the child? Is the injury consistent with the manner in which it reportedly was sustained? Is there personal or family medical history pertinent to the findings? Is the description of the traumatic event plausible and consistent on repetition by one

(a)

(b)

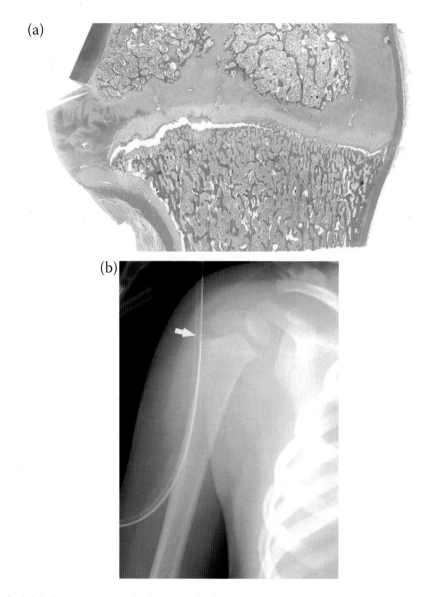

Figure 2.6 (a) Photomacrograph showing the location of the classic metaphyseal lesion (CML) in the most immature ossified portion of the metaphysis lying just beneath the cartilaginous growth plate. (b) Radiograph of the same bone with CML (arrow). (Courtesy Andrew Baker, MD. With permission. All rights reserved.)

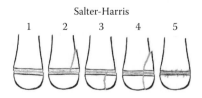

Salter-Harris

1   2   3   4   5

Figure 2.7 Schematic drawing of the location of the five types of Salter-Harris fractures of the physis and adjacent epiphysis or metaphysis. Type 1 is through the physis. Type 2 also involves the metaphysis. Type 3 extends into the epiphysis. Type 4 involves the physis, metaphysis, and epiphysis. Type 5 is a crush injury to the physis or growth plate.

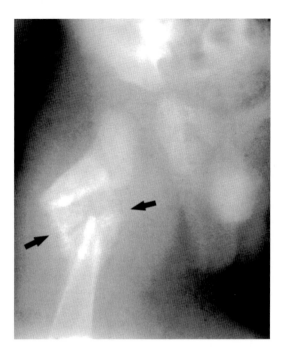

Figure 2.8 Badly displaced transverse fracture of the proximal femoral shaft with no immobilization. Note the massive periosteal new bone produced as a result (arrows).

or several witnesses? Is there social history suggestive of provocative stress, previous abuse, or frequent injury in the family?

A fine distinction can be made as to whether a nonaccidental injury was intentional or nonintentional, the latter situation implying neglect, which is only abuse of a different kind. We would suggest that the broad differentiation—accidental or nonaccidental—will suffice as the focus of this book and of the first responder. The finer distinction can be left to legal dispute.

Part 2: Radiological Findings in Nonaccidental Trauma

Introduction

The importance of demonstrable skeletal lesions in the diagnosis of child abuse has been appreciated since the earliest awareness of the problem. However, even in cases positively identified as victims of physical abuse, fewer than one-third are found to have skeletal injury.[16] On the other hand, of children initially presenting with skeletal injury, the percentage of those diagnostic for nonaccidental trauma is quite small, especially in children beyond 2 years of age.

The incidence, type, location, and significance of fractures is extremely age dependent in the abused child. Beyond infancy, fractures unassociated with other clinical evidence of inflicted trauma are very rare. A large multicenter study of abused children aged 3 weeks to 16 years[16] revealed that more than half of all fractures encountered involved infants (younger than 1 year). Children younger than 2 years accounted for 90% of all skull fractures. The CML, rib fractures, and fractures at multiple sites are present in infants fatally abused. Conversely, abused older children are more likely to have long-bone diaphyseal injuries.[17]

Fractures of the Appendicular Skeleton

Metaphyseal Injuries

In his first paper on what was to become known as child abuse or the battered child,[18] Caffey described multiple fractures in long bones, particularly noting unusual fractures with metaphyseal fragmentation. Thanks to Kleinman and co-workers, we now recognize these as the classic metaphyseal lesion (CML) of nonaccidental trauma to the infant and very young child. The fracture through the immature spongiosa at the extreme end of the growing metaphysis (previously described) creates a disk of bone, usually a bit thinner centrally than at its periphery. How this fragment is perceived on a radiograph depends on the angle of the central x-ray beam to the fracture and to some extent on technical factors (i.e., contrast and density) (Figure 2.9). Thus, whether perceived as a "corner fracture," a "bucket-handle fracture," as a disk of bone, or (rarely) as a straight transverse fracture, it is the same injury.

Although not the most common fracture in child abuse, the CML is the most specific. It is found in one-half or fewer of cases younger than 24 months of age, and quite rarely beyond that age. CMLs are found most commonly in the distal femur (Figure 2.10) and, in descending order of frequency, the proximal tibia (Figure 2.11), the distal tibia (Figure 2.12), and the proximal humerus (Figure 2.13), but can occur at either end of any long bone (Figure 2.14). The transverse shearing force at the epiphyseal-metaphyseal junction is thought to occur

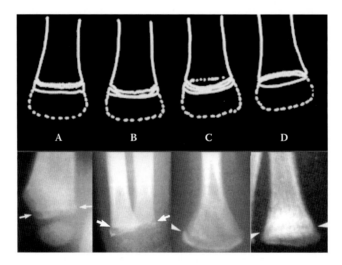

Figure 2.9 Top: Schematic drawing of how a classic CML can appear as a result of a slight alteration in the relative position of the bone to the central x-ray beam: (a) a transverse fracture, (b) corner fractures, (c) a bucket-handle fracture, (d) a disk of bone. Bottom: Representative radiographs. (Drawings from Brogdon, B.G., in Spitz, W.V., and Spitz, D.J., eds., *Medicolegal Investigation of Death*, 4th ed., CC Thomas, Springfield, IL, 2006, chap. 6. With permission. Radiograph from Thali, M.J., et al., eds., *Brogdon's Forensic Radiology*, 2nd ed., CRC Press, Boca Raton, FL, 2010. With permission.)

from to-and-fro manipulation of the extremity as a handle, or by the violent flailing of the extremities, as the baby is gripped around the chest and vigorously shaken.[17,19]

In the essentially nonmobile infant or child, the CML often is clinically occult. It tends to heal with little or no callus or periosteal reaction. Consequently, they are difficult to age or date. They produce little if any long-term deformity or other effect if the child survives its abusive travail.[13]

Caffey, later in his Mackenzie Davidson Memorial Lecture,[19] spoke of "metaphyseal cupping." These lesions appear to represent post-traumatic cessation or retardation of growth, producing a smaller epiphyseal center "cupped" in a narrow growth plate at the end of a shortened bone (Figure 2.15). Caffey also described at this time "ectopic ossification centers," a complete traumatic epiphyseal-diaphyseal dislocation (Figure 2.16).

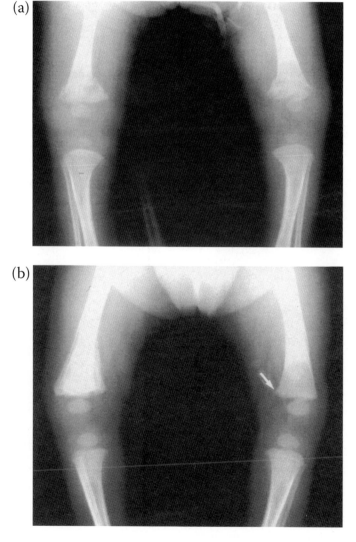

Figure 2.10 (a) Bilateral knees show large corner fractures in the distal femoral metaphyses. (b) Bilateral knees showing large corner fracture of the distal femoral metaphysis on the right (viewer left) with extensive subperiosteal new bone indicating that this injury is several days or weeks old. A small corner fracture on the left (arrow) is new.

(c)

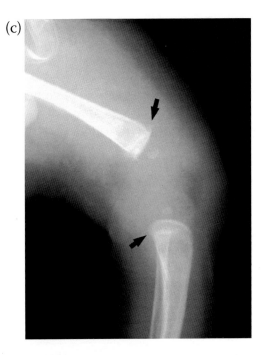

Figure 2.10 (*Continued*) (c) Acute corner fractures of the distal femur and proximal tibia in a newborn infant. Note the tiny secondary ossification centers of the femur and tibia.

(a)

(b)

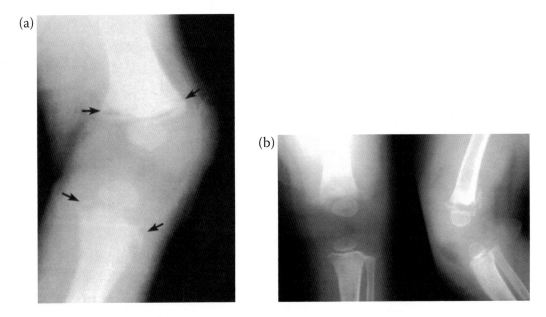

Figure 2.11 (a) Corner fractures (arrows) at both the distal femur and proximal tibial metaphysis. (b) Acute CML is barely apparent at the proximal tibia, while an older one at the distal femur is healing with periosteal new bone.

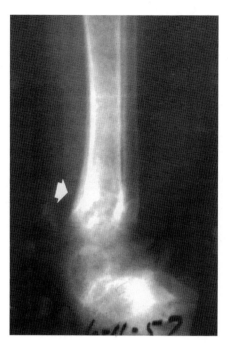

Figure 2.12 Healed angulated fracture of the distal tibial and fibular metaphyses.

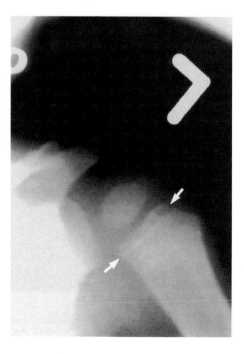

Figure 2.13 Transverse CML in the proximal humeral metaphysis. The central x-ray beam happens to be precisely parallel to the plane of the fractures.

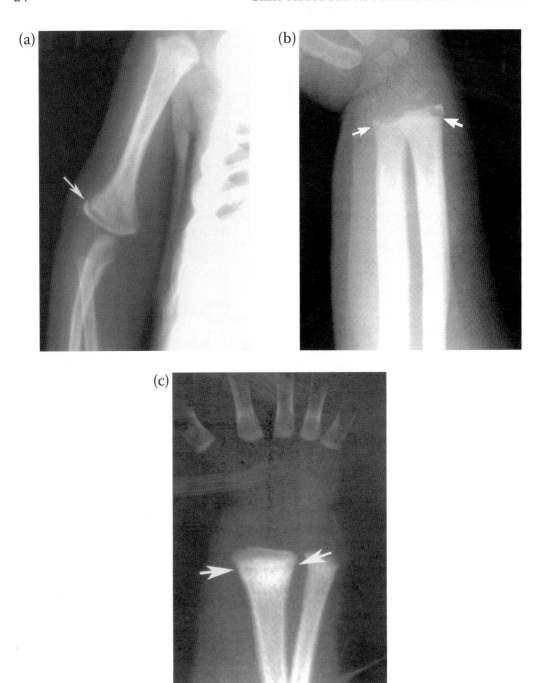

Figure 2.14 (a) Bucket-handle type CML at the distal humerus. (b) Corner fractures at the distal radius and ulna. (c) CML at the distal radius (arrows).

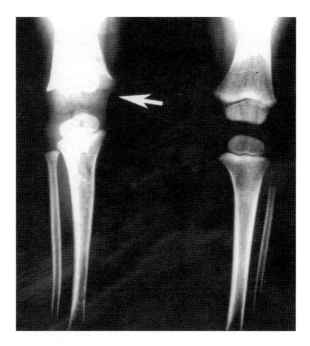

Figure 2.15 Example of what Caffey called metaphyseal cupping, actually a traumatic disturbance of the growth plate.

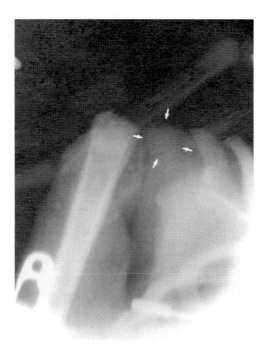

Figure 2.16 Caffey described this lesion as an ectopic ossification center. Actually, the secondary ossification center (for the head of the humerus) is properly located. The humeral shaft is displaced secondary to fracture through the physis—a complete traumatic epiphyseal-metaphyseal dislocation.

Diaphyseal (Shaft) Fractures

Diaphyseal fractures of long bones are common in both accidental and nonaccidental injuries of children beyond age 2. They will have different characteristics and appearances depending on the direction of force applied to the bone: transverse, oblique, spiral, the butterfly or wedge fragment, or shearing, as previously shown (Figure 2.4).

Transverse fractures are highly suspicious in the nonambulatory child, given no history of a massive traumatic event, i.e., motor vehicle accident or fall down stairs (Figure 2.17), but less so in the older child. They reflect a direct blow perpendicular to the long axis of the bone.

At one time spiral fractures were thought to be indicative of abuse, but they can occur from either accident or intent (Figure 2.18). They reflect a twisting or torsion stress to the bone. Oblique fractures similarly are inconclusive (Figure 2.19).

(a)

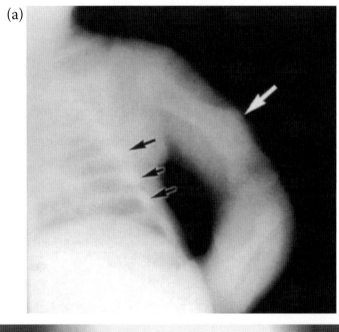

(b)

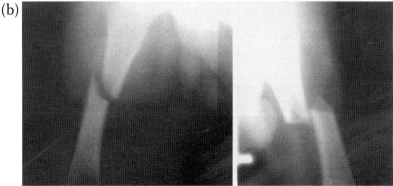

Figure 2.17 (a) Almost completely healed transverse fracture of the midhumeral shaft with some residual angulation (large arrows). Remodeling will eventually restore the bone to essentially normal configuration. Note the multiple healing lateral rib fractures, probably a bit more recently sustained (small arrows). (b) Bilateral displaced fractures of the proximal femora in a nonwalking child. The family, especially the father, had been stressed by an unexpected recall from an overseas diplomatic assignment.

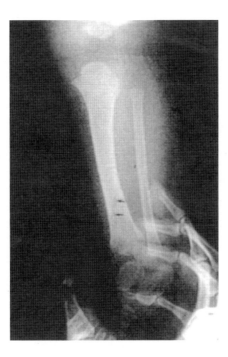

Figure 2.18 Undisplaced spiral fractures of the distal tibial shaft resembling a "toddler's fracture," but this infant is not yet walking.

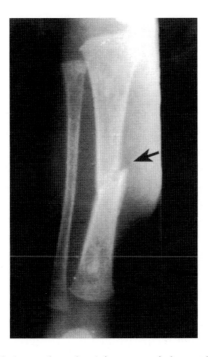

Figure 2.19 Relatively fresh (1 week or less) fracture of the mid-diaphysis of the tibia with slight displacement and overriding of fragments at the fracture site producing minimal bowing fracture of the fibula.

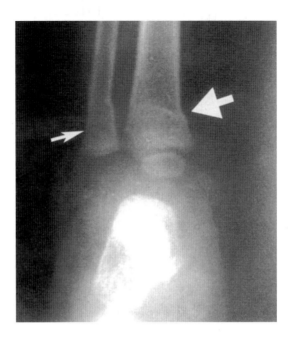

Figure 2.20 Caffey's "traumatic bowing of the ends of diaphyses due to metaphyseal infraction" now would be described as incomplete fractures at the metaphyseal-diaphyseal junction.

The combination of compression and bowing forces can produce the butterfly fragment, which may have forensic connotations but is not necessarily indicative of abuse
(Figure 2.4d).

Caffey's "traumatic bowing of the ends of diaphyses due to metaphyseal infraction"[20]
would now be reported as a bowing or incomplete fracture at the metaphyseal-diaphyseal
junction (Figure 2.20).

Rib Fractures

Rib fractures in older children and adults usually are caused by a direct blow to the area,[13]
which may be accidental (a fall, a motor vehicle accident) or inflicted (a fist, a weapon).
Ordinarily only one or a few ribs will be fractured, and with the exception of massive
trauma, they usually are unilateral.

Even in older children the remarkable plasticity of the ribs allows considerable deformation without fracture. We have reported a case in which the thorax of a 13-year-old was
passed over by a truck, producing a traumatic rupture of the interventricular septum but
no rib fracture.[21]

In the absence of metabolic disease and well-documented massive accidental trauma, rib
fractures in infants and young children are highly specific for physical abuse. Most are produced by a specific mechanism: The tiny chest is encircled by adult hands and tightly squeezed,
often while being shaken. When this manual compression and deformation of the thorax
exceeds the malleability of the ribs, fractures can occur at different locations[22] (Figure 2.21).

Posterior fractures are most frequent. The rib is firmly attached to the vertebral body
and the transverse process (Figure 2.22). Squeezing compression levers the posterior area
of the rib over the transverse process; cortical fracture begins on the ventral surface and
can progress to complete fracture just lateral to the tip of the transverse process.[13,23] These
fractures so close to the costotransverse process articulation are difficult to see in the acute

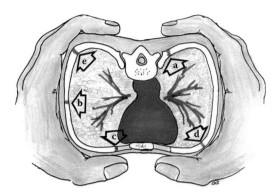

Figure 2.21 Schematic illustration of rib fractures resulting from grasping the small chest with two adult hands, then squeezing or shaking it. (a) Most common fracture site, posterior, just lateral to the budding transverse process of vertebrae. (b) Lateral rib fractures, although less common, ordinarily are more easily detected (see Figure 2.23a) but can be missed when acute and nondisplaced (see Figure 2.23b). (c) Front-to-back pressure on the rib cage can produce anterior rib fractures at or near the costochondral junction. These produce less callus when healing, and consequently may be difficult to detect. (d) Anterolateral rib fractures are not as common as their posterior counterparts but usually are readily detected.

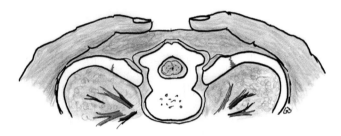

Figure 2.22 Schematic drawing showing how the common posterior rib fracture is produced by levering over the fulcrum of the vertebral transverse process. The structural failure begins at the anterior cortical surface and progresses from anterior to posterior.

stage on the usual anteroposterior frontal radiograph. They become more obvious, of course, as the usually abundant callus is formed and becomes more calcified (Figure 2.23). Posterior oblique views of the chest will improve visualization of fractures in this location.

Radionuclide scintiscans are more sensitive than radiography for early detection of rib fractures but are impractical for first-encounter evaluations, often being unavailable 24/7, and the results are not immediately available in any case (Figure 2.24). The increased takeup of radionuclides at the growth plate of long bones complicates evaluation of possible CMLs (Figure 2.25).

Although less common, lateral fractures of ribs ordinarily are more easily detected (Figure 2.26). Still, if undisplaced, lateral fractures can be overlooked (Figure 2.27).

Front-to-back pressure on the chest may cause anterior fractures as the costochondral junction is pushed inward. These fractures are difficult to detect when fresh and may not produce as many calluses when healing as fractures in other locations (see Figure 2.21).

Rib fractures are more common than long-bone fractures in child abuse because they are usually multiple, bilateral, and relatively symmetrical (Figure 2.25). If rib fractures are detected radiographically, it is highly likely that there are others present but unseen.

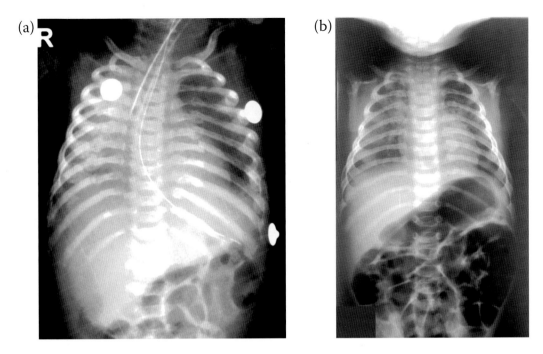

Figure 2.23 (a) Multiple bilateral rib fractures, with callus, are easily seen, as are the healing lateral rib fractures on the left. (b) Undisplaced posterior rib fractures may be partially obscured by cardiac and mediastinal shadows.

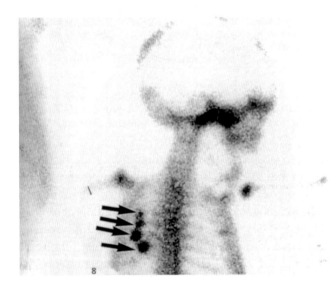

Figure 2.24 Nuclear bone scan reveals multiple rib fractures (arrows) not yet seen on conventional radiographs.

High-detail radiography is essential. One investigation of fatal inflicted abuse showed that 51% of total fractures found involved ribs, but only 36% of those rib fractures were visible on skeletal survey.[24]

Rib fractures in infants and young children apparently are relatively asymptomatic, as symptoms or complications are absent in about 80%. Thus most are not diagnosed

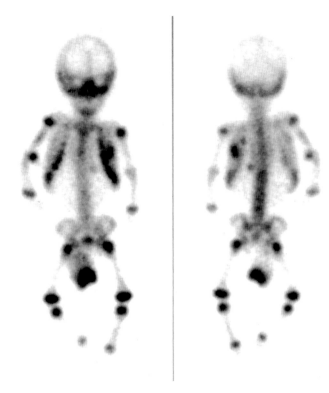

Figure 2.25 Anterior and posterior whole-body nuclear bone scans show multiple rib fractures, both front and back. Note the normal increased uptake at the growing ends of long bones, which makes symmetrical CMLs quite difficult to appreciate, thus limiting the reliability of this study. The high uptake at the right elbow represents the injection site.

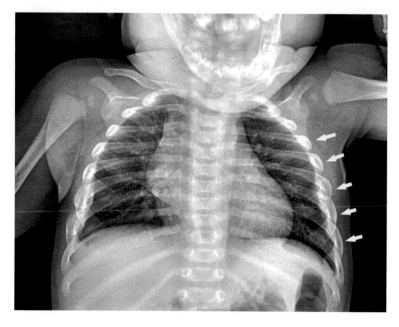

Figure 2.26 Bilateral healed lateral rib fractures (arrows).

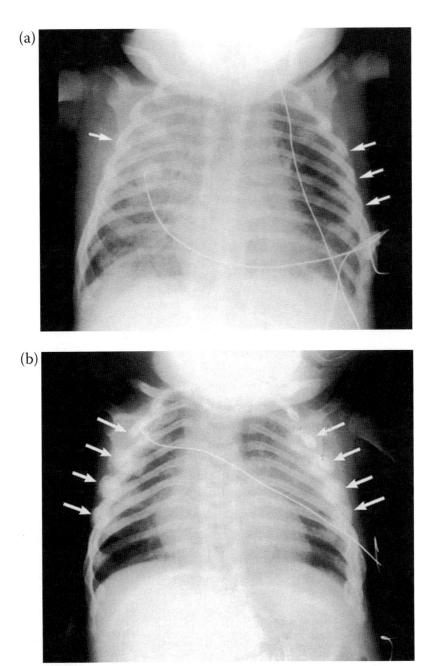

Figure 2.27 (a) A few acute undisplaced lateral rib fractures are barely discernable. (b) As healing progressed with abundant callus they become obvious.

primarily.[13] Bruising or hematomas in the shape of fingerprints can be an important clue to underlying fractures.

Fractures of the first rib are virtually pathognosnomic of inflicted trauma (Figure 2.28).

Focal, asymmetric, unilateral rib fractures result from direct impact and suggest a possible blow from a fist or weapon (Figure 2.29) but may also be accidental, as by a fall upon an object or in bones weakened by metabolic processes.

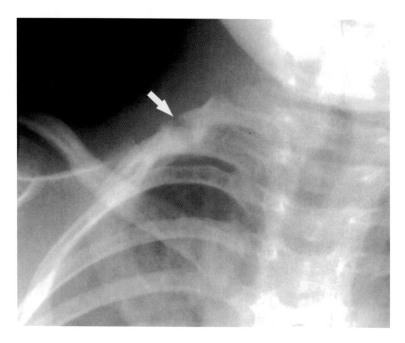

Figure 2.28 Healing first rib fracture appears to be developing a nonunion. Abuse likely at this location.

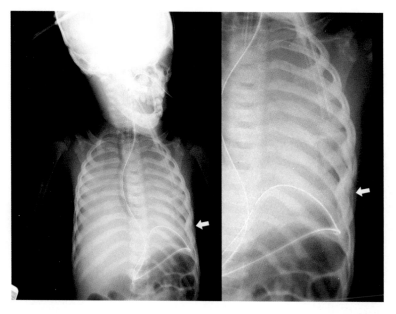

Figure 2.29 Unilateral focal rib fractures (arrow) probably caused by a direct blow.

Intrapartum rib fractures are extremely rare, being reported in instances of large fetuses, difficult deliveries, or both.[13] In one study of 34,940 live births, there were no rib fractures during delivery.[25]

Cardiopulmonary resuscitation is an extraordinarily unlikely cause for rib fracture in children. Maguire and co-workers[26] found anterior rib fractures in only 3 of 923 children who underwent CPR rendered by both trained and untrained persons. There were no posterior rib fractures!

The Scapula

Because of its location, covered by layers of muscle, the scapula is rarely fractured in children. Scapula fractures result from direct impact, which usually is plausibly explained by a fall, auto accident, blow from a bat, etc. When a scapular fracture is found in a child in the absence of such an incident, then abusive inflicted trauma is highly suspect.[27] The acromion is the common site for scapular fracture (Figure 2.30). The coracoid process is fractured less commonly. Besides direct blows, scapular fractures may occur from shaking or when the arm is pulled with great violence or forced behind the child's back.[13] When a scapular fracture is identified, other parts of that bone should be checked carefully for additional fractures. However, the developing scapula has multiple secondary ossification centers that may mimic a fracture. Acute fractures have sharply defined margins without sclerotic margins. Ossification centers will have a dense zone of provisional calcification at their margins.

The Sternum

Sternum fractures are rare in children and lacking a history of accident have a high specificity for child abuse.[28–30] Fractures can be sustained from a direct blow and may be associated with dislocation, particularly at the sternal angle. They are difficult to detect on conventional AP and lateral radiographs. They are not to be expected from cardiopulmonary resuscitation on a child.

Hands and Feet

Except for the occasional fracture of the distal phalanx of fingers caught in a closing door, hand fractures are suspicious for inflicted trauma (Figure 2.31). They accounted for only 4% of fractures in the series of Kleinman et al. already cited.[17]

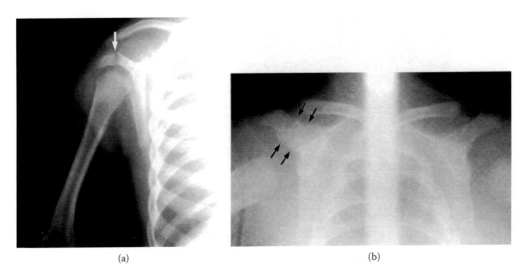

(a)   (b)

Figure 2.30 (a) Acute undisplaced fracture of the acromion. (b) Healed acromial fracture with abundant mature callus.

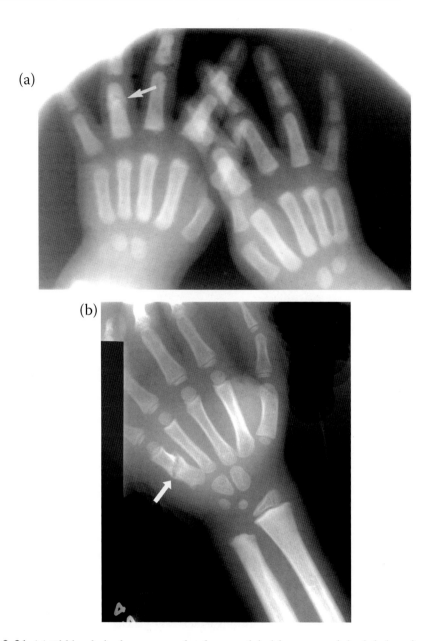

Figure 2.31 (a) Old healed, almost completely remodeled fractures of the left fourth proximal phalanx. This is the same child shown in Figures 2.13 and 2.16. Each of these injuries occurred at a different time but all were detected on a single visit. (b) Healing fracture of the left fifth metacarpal in a 4-year-old (same case as Figure 2.37a).

Abusive fractures of the feet are even less common, but we have seen a case where the toes were burned off a child when an abusive parent literally "held her feet to the fire" (Figure 2.32).

Clavicle

Clavicular fractures are the most common perinatal or intraparium fracture usually, but not always, occurring in the mid-shaft. They are commonly acquired during the normal

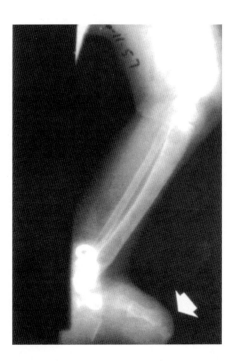

Figure 2.32 This 11-month-old girl from a hippie commune literally had her foot held to the fire until her toes were burned off.

activities of the healthy, mobile child. As an isolated finding they have a low specificity for abuse (Figure 2.33). They frequently are discovered only because of the palpable mass of their healing callus or, less commonly, malunion or nonunion (Figure 2.33).

Multiple Fractures of Different Ages

Again, first mentioned by Caffey,[20] multiple fractures in various stages of healing have a high specificity for child abuse if there is an absence of or inconsistent history of multiple accidents (Figure 2.34). In a series of 165 fractures in 31 infants who died of child abuse,[17] all but two had at least one healing fracture.

Dislocations of the Appendicular Skeleton

True dislocation or subluxation of joints is exceedingly rare in the peak age range for child abuse (except in the spine, described later). These are most often suspected at the shoulder and hip, where the ligament(s) attaching the proximal epiphysis of the long bone to its articular counterpart is stronger than the physis. Consequently, a "pseudodislocation" is produced,[31] which actually is a fracture. The axis of the long bone will appear to be, and is, displaced from its usual relationship to the scapula or pelvis. But the proximal epiphysis remains in normal position (Figures 2.16 and 2.35). This may be unappreciated or unseen if the epiphyseal center is not yet ossified, quite small, or faintly opacified. Similar caution must be exercised in the diagnosis of dislocation at other joints.[32] If doubtful, ultrasonography is helpful in locating and showing the true position of a unopacified epiphysis.

So-called nursemaid's elbow is a partial anterior subluxation of the radial head, commonly seen in infants and children up to age 4. It results from pulling upon or lifting the child

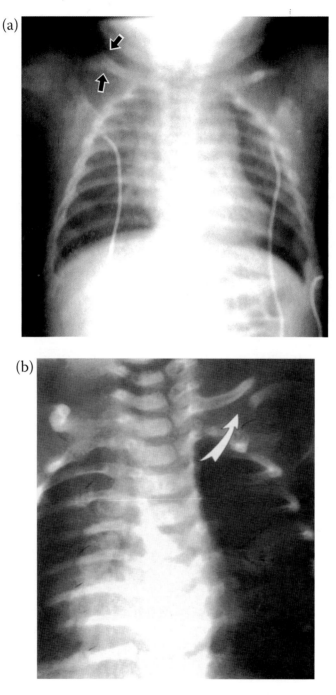

Figure 2.33 (a) Healing fracture of the right clavicle palpated on routine well-baby examination. Not abuse. (b) Old nonunion of the left clavicle discovered on chest radiographs obtained for an unrelated indication. Not abuse.

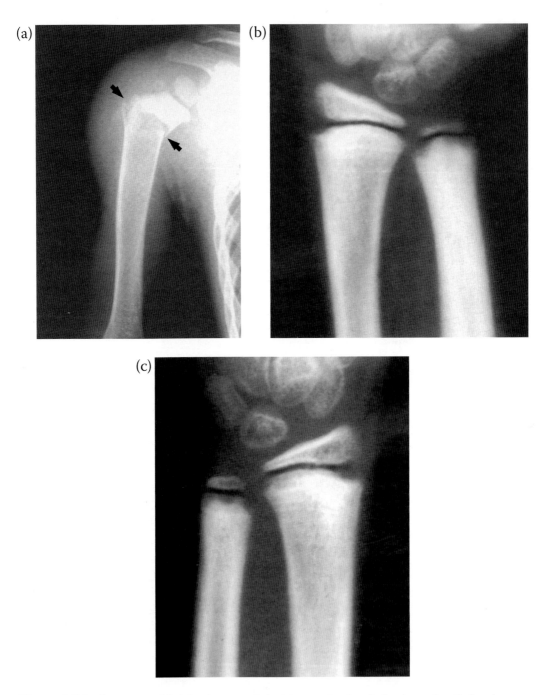

Figure 2.34 This 7-year-old girl volunteered the history that her father beats her "when he gets drunk." (a) Recent fracture of the proximal humeral metaphysis with minimal displacement and no callus. (b) Bilateral growth plate injuries to the distal left radius and ulna. (c) Bilateral growth plate injuries to the distal right radius and ulna.

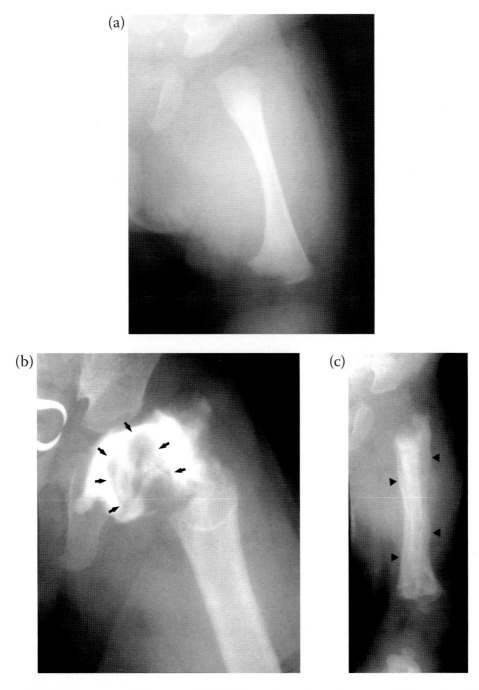

Figure 2.35 (a) Apparent dislocation of the left hip of an infant whose capital femoral epiphysis is not yet ossified. (b) Contrast injection of the hip joint shows the unossified epiphysis to be properly located in the acetabulum. There is separation and lateral displacement of the femoral shaft at the level of the physis. There is some periosteal reaction along the proximal femoral shaft first thought to be post-traumatic, but the joint became infected. (c) Blighted development of the proximal epiphysis.

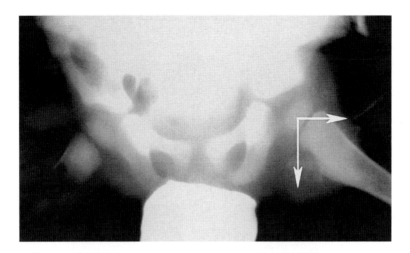

Figure 2.36 Subluxation of the left hip due to intracapsular blood or effusion in a child who had massive trauma elsewhere. This child probably was swung by this extremity. Compare with the normal right hip.

by an extended arm. Episodes may be as innocent as pulling an arm through a sleeve or assisting the child to turn over.[33] It is easily diagnosed upon physical examination and rarely requires imaging (ultrasonography will do nicely). It is not indicative of child abuse.

True subluxation can occur, again almost exclusively at the hip or shoulder, due to trauma or displacement of the epiphyseal end of the long bone by large collections of fluid, blood, or pus within the joint capsule (Figure 2.36). Widening of the joint space in the shoulder also can come from muscular laxity secondary to brachial plexus injury.[32]

Periosteal Reactions

Caffey described "involucrum" in his 1946 paper,[18] borrowing a term long in use to describe a finding in the common condition of osteomyelitis in pre-antibiotic decades (Figure 2.26). The infection in either the spongiosa or medulla of a bone would break through the cortex, spreading pus beneath, and elevating the periosteum. This results in a "sleeve" of new bone (called the involucrum) around the original confines of the cortex. After portions of the cortical bone become necrotic, avascular, and dead, the dead bone, appearing more dense than the diseased, osteoporotic, living bone, was called sequestrum.

When the thick, reactive periosteum of the child is separated from the underlying bone by shearing torsional forces or by the collection of blood or pus, the production of subperiosteal new bone will be stimulated (Figure 2.37). This will be radiographically discernable in about 7 days. Repetitive insults will create multiple layers of new bone (lamellar periostitis). Periosteal new bone in the absence of fracture, and when cutaneous lesions are absent or have disappeared, can be the first indicator of physical abuse (Figures 2.38 and 2.39).

With undisplaced fractures, blood will collect beneath the stripped but intact periosteum and will help support the fragments in position. Disruption of the periosteum is a prerequisite for displacement of fractures. Disruption may increase periosteal new bone formation, as will nonimmobilization of fractures and some pre-existing conditions of the bony skeleton.

Healing of periosteal reactions is a gradual process of consolidation with the underlying bone. Many factors can affect the rate of healing—age, general health, immobilization,

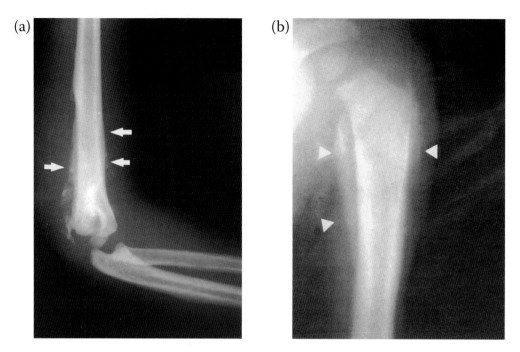

Figure 2.37 (a) Four-year-old with fracture-dislocation of the elbow. Note the extensive calcification of subperiosteal and para-articular hematoma (same case as Figure 2.31a). (b) Calcifying subperiosteal hematoma due to stippling of the periosteum from the bone by torsion (arrows). No fracture.

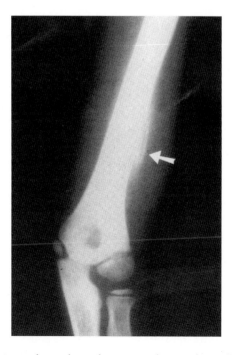

Figure 2.38 Focal subperiosteal new bone formation from a direct blow. Same child as shown in Figure 2.34.

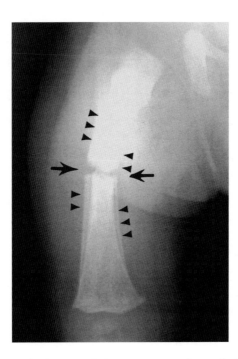

Figure 2.39 Torsional forces had stripped the periosteum from the bone. Subperiosteal blood had calcified in a single layer. A subsequent transverse fracture of the femur involved both the bone and the unilaminar periosteal calcification, indicating multiple traumatic events on a single radiograph. (From Rich, J., *Forensic Medicine of the Lower Extremity*, Humana Press, Totowa, NJ, 2005, p. 179, Figure 50. With permission of Springer Science+Business Media.)

intercurrent disease, or repetitive injury—so timing of initial injury by periosteal healing is imprecise, and particularly so, in the child.[34]

Fractures of the Axial Skeleton

The Spine

Fractures of the spine are rare in children, requiring high-energy contact trauma applied to a relatively small surface. Traffic accidents are the most common cause overall and predominate particularly in children 2 years of age or below. Falls are a more prevalent cause of spinal injury between ages 2 and 9 years. From 9 to 15 years sports injuries predominate.[32] Absent any history of plausible trauma, bone disease, or no history at all, a pediatric spinal fracture is highly suggestive for inflicted trauma and usually will be found in association with other lesions indicating abuse. Even when the diagnosis of physical child abuse is established, the incidence of spinal involvement is extremely low, 3% or less.[35–39]

Swischuk,[40] more than two decades after Caffey's initial paper, was first to study spinal injuries from child abuse. He collected six cases that essentially described the spectrum of injuries of that etiology:

1. The anterior notch or a wedge, a compression of the anterosuperior corner of the vertebral body as seen in lateral projection (Figure 2.40).
2. Compression of both superior and inferior end plates producing a more pointed shape to the vertebral body (Figure 2.41). If the end plates are symmetrically

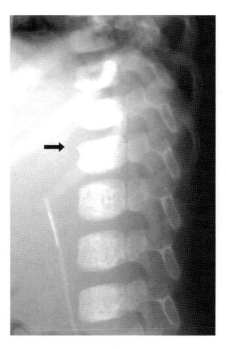

Figure 2.40 Typical small anterior notch, or wedge, representing a minimal compression of the anterosuperior corner of the vertebral body (arrow). (Courtesy G.J. Lonergan, MD.)

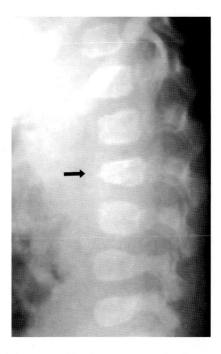

Figure 2.41 Compression deformity of both superior and inferior corners of the vertebral body (arrow). (From Lonergan, G.J., et al., *Radiographics* 2003; 23:811–45. With permission.)

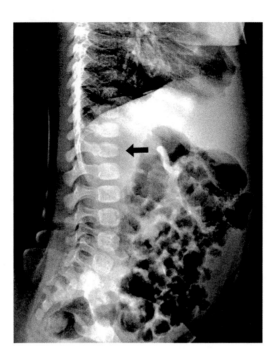

Figure 2.42 Symmetrical flattening of both end plates of the vertebral body. If severely flattened, this is termed a *vertebra plana*. (Courtesy G.J. Lonergan, MD.)

compressed, a flattened vertebral body will result (vertebra plana) (Figure 2.42). A few may show end plate fractures without compression.[41]

3. Fracture-dislocation or subluxation with fracture, or transient dislocation without fracture but with spinal cord injury. The latter situation is now known as SCIWORA (spinal cord injury without radiological abnormality).[42] This is a rather unfortunate acronym. It should be SCIWORF (spinal cord injury without radiological fracture). Although these are abnormalities that may be seen without *fracture*, more subtle abnormalities may be present. Swischuk, in his case #VI with cord swelling from edema or hematoma despite no fractures, noted telltale widening of paravertebral soft tissues. He correctly deduced that there must have been dislocation with spontaneous reduction.[41]

Vertebral fractures result from flexion-extension stresses. *Fracture-dislocation* in the spine is not likely accidental unless from an unambiguous massive trauma event. It is more likely the result of an inflicted direct blow (Figure 2.43), violent shaking with to-and-fro flexion and extension, whiplashing as the child is thrown into space and jerked back, or simply slammed down on his or her bottom (Figure 2.44) or against a wall or other solid object (Figure 2.45).

The unusually elastic biomechanics of the pediatric spine allow traumatic deformations beyond physiologic limits, permitting spinal cord trauma from hyperextension/ flexion, longitudinal distraction, or vascular compromise, followed by spontaneous reduction of the spinal displacement. In the absence of fracture, this may only be apparent radiographically by lateral subluxation (Figure 2.45), paraspinous soft tissue widening (Figure 2.46), or increased separation of spinous processes on either AP or lateral

(a) (b)

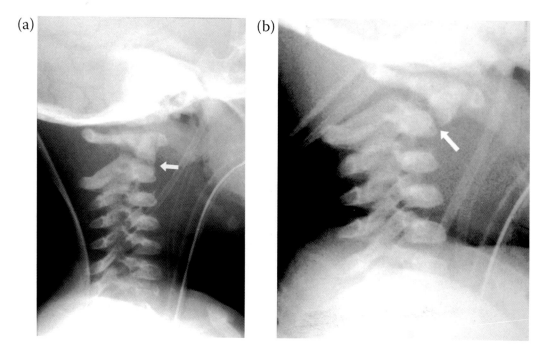

Figure 2.43 This child was struck heavily on the back of the head. (a) On the initial study, the fracture at the base of the odontoid process (arrow) was not appreciated. The wide separation of the spinous processes of C1 and C2 should have aroused concern. (b) A later study of this child, who had not been immobilized in the interval, shows a marked C1-C2 dislocation (arrow).

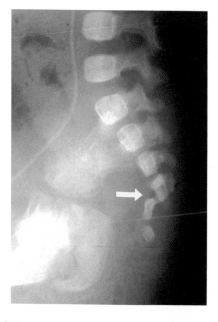

Figure 2.44 Dislocation of the sacrum at S4-S5 caused by slamming the baby down on its bottom. (From Lonergan, G.J., et al., *Radiographics* 2003; 23:811–45. With permission.)

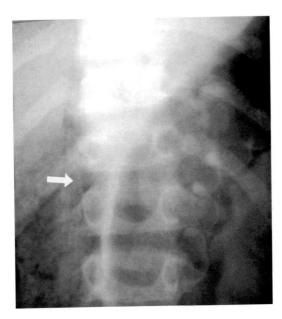

Figure 2.45 This baby, slammed against a wall, sustained a lateral subluxation of T12 on L1 (arrow).

projections (Figure 2.47). In children the separation of the usual spinous processes of C1 and C2 can be somewhat variable on the routine cross-table lateral projection. If in doubt go immediately to CT. At other levels the separation should not be appreciably different from that of the spine above and below. Symptoms of spinal cord injury may be delayed and, when apparent, may call for intensive further investigation with sectional imaging studies (CT and MRI).

Fortunately for diagnostic purposes, any case of multiple skeletal injuries is an indication for careful, intensive, and sophisticated radiological examination of the spine.

The Skull

Fractures: Accidental or Abusive?

Incidence and Significance Skull fractures of either accidental or nonaccidental origin can occur in infants and children of any age. However, the ratio of fractures due to abuse versus those that are accident related is roughly inversely related to the age of the child. Thus only about 12% of all physically abused children suffer a skull fracture, but the incidence rises to 80–95% of abused infants less than 1 year of age.[43–45] Ergo abuse is the commonest cause of serious head injury in infants and the commonest cause of death in those victims. Therefore any head injury in the infant or young child, in the absence of a high-impact accident or other major trauma, warrants an abuse investigation.[45]

The skull of the infant/child with its thin bones and open sutures responds to trauma quite differently than does the adult calvaria.[47] Fractures of the immature skull result from two different types of stresses: (1) *static loading* from a relatively slow impact with pressure applied over time (i.e., squeezing, wedging between unyielding surfaces, childbirth) can

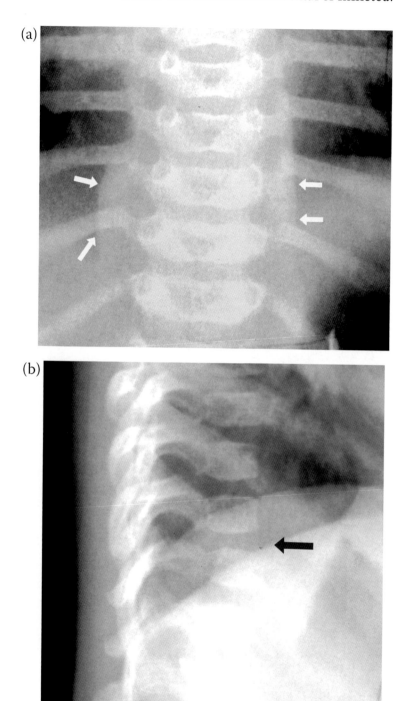

Figure 2.46 (a) Although the spinal alignment appears normal in this frontal view, the widening of the paraspinal soft tissue by hematoma (arrows) indicates further study. (b) Lateral view of the same child shows posterior subluxation of T10 on T11 (arrow).

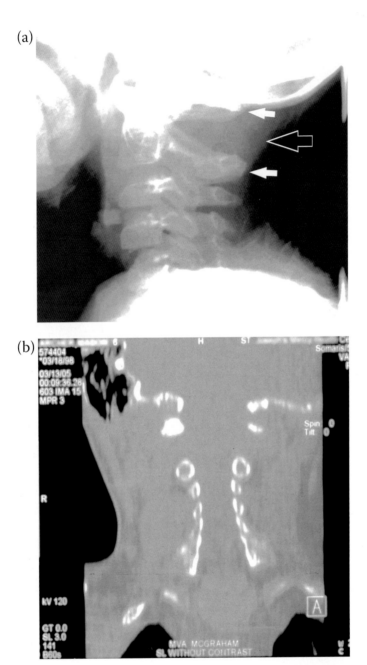

Figure 2.47 (a) The cross-table lateral view of the cervical spine of this 6-year-old male involved in a motor vehicle accident was interpreted as normal despite the widening of the C1-C2 (white arrows) interspinous distance (hollow arrow). He later became unable to move his toes or to void. (b) Coronal reconstruction of his CT shows the wide separation of the lateral masses of C1 and C2. Traction on the spinal cord had produced a tear and hemorrhage at the level of T1-T2 with subsequent paraplegia—a case of SCIWORF (see text).

cause focal injury, such as a linear fracture in one bone, or occasionally, multiple fractures; and (2) *dynamic loading*, which can be accidental or intentional. There are two types:

1. Impulse loading: Acceleration/deceleration head movement without impact or fractures—hence not applicable to fracture issues, but possibly pertinent to the so-called shaken baby syndrome (see below).
2. Impact loading involves context in one of four situations: (i) head stationary, object moves; (ii) head moves, object stationary; (iii) head moves, object moves in opposing directions, or (iv) in the same direction at different velocities.

Impact injuries usually injure one or more soft tissue layers overlying the bony skull, but the location of these superficial lesions may not correlate with an underlying skull fracture. In studying the external lesions of children with skull fractures, Harwood-Nash et al. found that 84% of fractures were ipsilateral, but 16% were contralateral.[48]

Types of Fractures by Etiology

Skull fractures secondary to mild or moderate accidental trauma typically are linear, undisplaced, undepressed, unilateral, parietal, and without associated subdural hematoma[46] (Figure 2.48).

Skull fractures secondary to abuse are more likely to be bilateral (Figure 2.49), comminuted (Figure 2.50), depressed (Figure 2.51), and wider than 1 mm (Figure 2.52); involve nonparietal bones and cross sutures; and are associated with other injuries, especially subdural hematoma or other intracranial injury. Consequently, neurological findings are most strongly associated with intentional trauma.[46,47,49]

Falls

The incidence of significant head injury from accidental falls is increased, of course, with the mobility and activity of the child. The unattended infant may roll off a bed, a couch, or a changing table, but these short-distance falls of a meter or so are highly unlikely to cause more damage than the occasional unilateral simple fracture, usually in a parietal bone. The more serious accidental injuries in this age group are encountered when the infant falls in or from the arms of his or her caretaker,[47,49–51] falls from a bunk bed, falls in a baby walker down stairs, falls on an irregular surface or object, or falls from great heights.[47]

Diagnostic Strategy

The initial search for skull fractures is best undertaken with conventional radiography since the plane of a CT slice may be parallel to the fracture. Of course this problem can be overcome if the initial CT thin-section scan is reformatted for 3D inspection. Evaluation of intracranial injury by sectional imaging is beyond the scope of this book. Overall there is poor correlation between skull fracture and underlying brain injury. Skull fracture is present in only 25–50% of cases with intracranial findings because of the plastic nature of the infantile skull.[52] Suffice it to say that intracranial injury is more common in inflicted trauma excepting massive traumatic events such as vehicular accidents.

Facial Fractures

Fractures of the facial bones of infants and children are an uncommon result of either accidental or nonaccidental trauma (Figures 2.53 and 2.54). Only 5% of all facial fractures

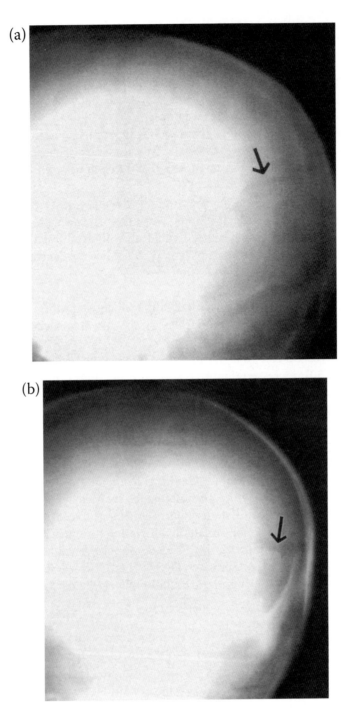

Figure 2.48 (a, b) Simple linear parietal skull fracture (arrows).

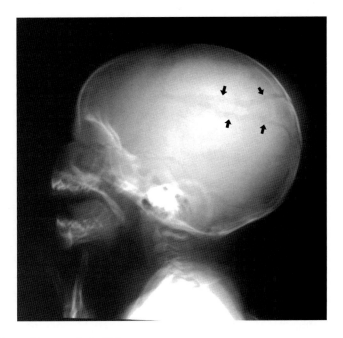

Figure 2.49 Bilateral parietal skull fracture.

(a)

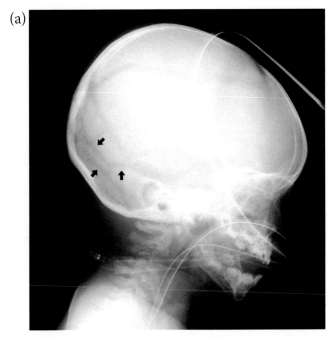

Figure 2.50 Comminuted skull fracture. Highly suggestive of abuse unless dependable history of massive accidental injury, i.e., motor vehicle accident.

(b)

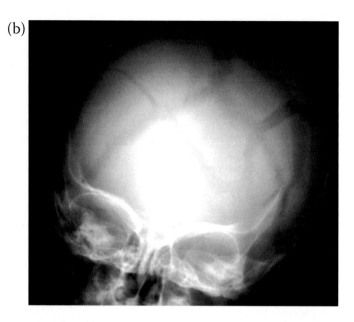

Figure 2.50 (*Continued*) Comminuted skull fracture. Highly suggestive of abuse unless dependable history of massive accidental injury, i.e., motor vehicle accident.

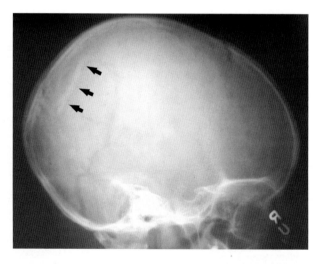

Figure 2.51 Depressed skull fracture. The edge of the depressed fragment (arrows) creates a linear increased density on the radiograph.

are found in children below age 12 and only 1% in preschool ages. The most common facial fracture resulting from physical abuse involves the mandible.[52]

Shaken Baby Syndrome

It has been established that rotational acceleration-deceleration is the leading biomechanical explanation for subdural hematoma in the shaken baby syndrome. Sudden changes in rotational motion cause shearing stress between brain and skull since they are rotating at

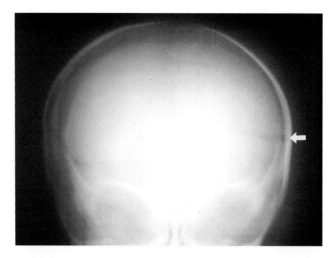

Figure 2.52 Linear skull fracture wider than 1 mm, suggesting possible increased intracranial pressure.

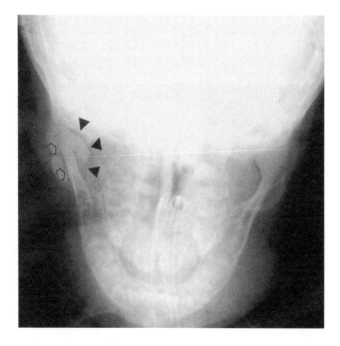

Figure 2.53 Fracture of the neck of the mandible with angulation, probably nonaccidental (arrowheads indicate displaced mandibular head). (Courtesy Drs. A.M. Kroman and S.A. Symes.)

different velocities. Bridging veins between those structures and within the brain itself are disrupted with subsequent intracranial bleeding. There are research-based arguments that rotational motion alone will not produce these injuries, that there must be impact as well.[55] Since there may be no external evidence of impact, this issue of causation by shaking alone versus shaking with impact is unresolved[13] (Figure 2.55).

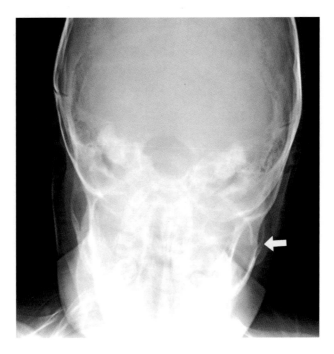

Figure 2.54 Fracture of the zygomatic arch, probably nonaccidental.

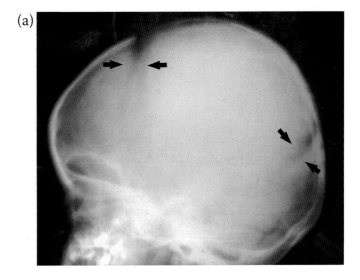

Figure 2.55 "Shaken baby" with no obvious fracture but massive separation of sutures. (a) Coronal and lambdoid.

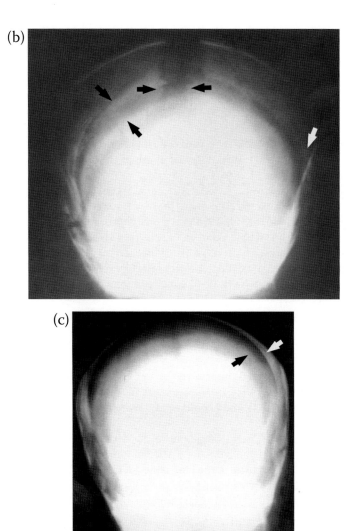

Figure 2.55 (*Continued*) "Shaken baby" with no obvious fracture but massive separation of sutures. (b) Sagittal, coronal, and squamosal. (c) Coronal.

References

1. Landin, L.A. 1983. Fracture patterns in children. Analysis of 8,682 fractures with spinal reference to incidence, etiology, and secular changes in a Swedish urban population 1950–1979. *Octa Orthop Scand Suppl* 202:100–9.
2. Landin, L.A. 1997. Epidemiology of children's fractures. *J Pediatr Orthop* B6:79–83.
3. Warlock, P., Stower, M., and Barbor, P. 1986. Patterns of fracture in accidental and non-accidental injuries in children: A comparative study. *Br Med J* 12:100–2.

4. Wilkins, K.E., and Aroojis, A.J. 2001. The present status of children's fractures. In Beaty, J.H., and Kasser, J.M., eds., *Rockwood and Wilkin's fractures in children*, 5th ed. Lippincott Williams & Wilkins, 3–20.

5. Bilo, R.A.C., Robbin, S.G., and van Rijn, R.R. 2010. *Forensic aspects of paediatric fractures*. Springer, Berlin, 1–13.

6. McMahon, P., Grossman, W., Gaffney, M., et al. 1995. Soft tissue injury as an indication of child abuse. *J Bone Jt Surg* 77:1179–83.

7. Cramer, K.E. 1996. Orthopaedic aspects of child abuse. *Pediatr Clin North Am* 43:1135–51.

8. Sinal, S.H., and Stewart, C.D. 1998. Physical abuse of children: A review for orthopedic surgeons. *J South Orthop Assoc* 7:264–70.

9. Kleinman, P.K., and Marks, S.C., Jr. 1996. A regional approach to the classic metaphyseal lesion in abused infants: The proximal humerus. *AJR Am J Roentgenol* 167:1399–403.

10. Kleinman, P.K., and Marks, S.C., Jr. 1996. A regional approach to the classic metaphyseal lesions in abused infants: The distal tibia. *AJR Am J Roentgenol* 166:1207–12.

11. Kleinman, P.K., and Marks, S.C., Jr. 1996. A regional approach to the classic metaphyseal lesion in abused infants: The proximal tibia. *AJR Am J Roentgenol* 166:421–26.

12. Kleinman, P.K., and Marks, S.C., Jr. 1998. A regional approach to the classic metaphyseal lesion in abused infants: The distal femur. *AJR Am J Roentgenol* 170:43–47.

13. Lonergan, G.J., Baker, A.M., Morey, M.K., and Boos, S.C. 2003. Child abuse: Radiologic-pathologic correlation. *Radiographics* 23:811–45.

14. Salter, R.B., and Harris, W.R. 1963. Injuries involving the epiphyseal plate. *J Bone Jr Surg A* 45:487–622.

15. Johnson, C.F. 1990. Inflicted injury versus accidental injury. *Pediatr Clin North Am* 37:791–814.

16. Merten, D.F., Radowski, M.A., and Leonidus, J.C. 1983. The abused child: A radiological reappraisal. *Radiology* 146:377–81.

17. Kleinman, P.K., Marks, S.C., and Blackbourne, B. 1995. The metaphysical lesion in abused infants: A radiologic-histopathologic study. *AJR Am J Roentgenol* 165:647–50.

18. Caffey, J. 1946. Multiple fractures in the long bones of infants suffering from chronic bubdural hematoma. *AJR Am J Roentgenol* 56:163–73.

19. Hymel, K.P., and Spirak, B.S. 2001. The biomechanics of physical injury. In Reese, R.M., and Ludwig, S., *Child abuse: Medical diagnosis and management*, 2nd ed. Lea and Febiger, Philadelphia, 1–22.

20. Caffey, J. 1957. Some traumatic lesions in growing bones other than fractures and dislocation, clinical and radiological fractures. *Br J Radiol* 30:225–38.

21. Crow, N.E., and Brogdon, B.G. 1959. Interventricular septal defect secondary to nonpenetrating injury. *Arch Internal Med* 103:791–95.

22. Bilo, R.A.C., Robbin, S.G., and van Rijn, R.R. 2010. *Forensic aspects of paediatric fractures*. Springer, Berlin, 49–68.

23. Kleinman, P.K., and Schlesinger, A.E. 1997. Mechanical factors associated with posterior rib fractures: Laboratory and clinical studies. *Pediatr Radiol* 27:87–91.

24. Kleinman, P.K., Marks, S.C., Nimkins, C., Rayder, S.M., and Kessler, S.C. 1996. Rib fractures in 31 abused infants: Postmortem radiologic-histopathologic study. *Radiology* 200:807–10.

25. Bhat, B.V., Kumar, V., and Oumachigui, A. 1994. Bone injuries during delivery. *Indian J Pediatr* 61:401–5.

26. Maguire, M., Mann, M., Ellaway, J.N., Siebert, J.R., and Kemp, A.M. 2006. Does cardiopulmonary resuscitation cause rib fractures? A systematic review. *Child Abuse Negl* 30:739–51.

27. Bilo, R.A.C., Robbin, S.G., and van Rijn, R.R. 2010. *Forensic aspects of paediatric fractures*. Springer, Berlin, 70–71.

28. Kogutt, M.S., Swischuk, L.E., and Fagan, C.J. 1974. Patterns of injury and significance of uncommon fractures in the battered child syndrome. *AJR Am J Roentgenol* 121:143–49.

29. Hobbs, C.J., Hanks, S.G.I., and Wynne, J.M. 1993. *Child abuse and neglect: A clinician's handbook*. Churchill Livingston, London, 57–65.

30. Kleinman, P.K. 1998. Skeletal trauma: General considerations. In Kleinman, P.K., *Diagnostic imaging of child abuse*, 2nd ed. Mosby, St. Louis, 8–25.

31. Kirks, D.R. 1992. Some unique aspects of pediatric fractures. In Harwood-Nash, D.C., and Patterson, H., *Pediatric radiology*. Merit Communications, London, 121–26.

32. Swrischuk, L.E. 1989. *Imaging of the newborn, infant, and young child*, 3rd ed. Williams & Wilkins, Baltimore, 731–36.

33. Schunk, J.E. 1990. Radial head subluxation: Epidemiology and treatment of 87 episodes. *Ann Emerg Med* 19:1019–23.

34. Hall C. 1994. Non-accidental injury. In Carty, H., Brunelle, F., Ringertz, H.G., Shaw, D., and Kendall, B., eds., *Imaging children*, vol. 2, Churchill Livingston, Edinburgh, 1188–202.

35. Bilo, R.A.C., Robbin, S.G., and van Rijn, R.R., 2010. *Forensic aspects of paediatric fractures*, Springer, Berlin, 44–74.

36. Cirak, B., Ziegfield, S., Knight, V.M., et al. 2004. Spinal injuries in children. *J Pediatr Surg* 39:607–12.

37. Bode, K.S., and Newton, P.O. 2007. Pediatric nonaccidental trauma thoracolumbar fracture-dislocation: Posterior spinal fusion with pedicle screw fixation in an 8-month-old boy. *Spine* 32:388–93.

38. Galleno, H., and Oppenheim, W.L. 1982. The battered child syndrome revisited. *Clin Orthop Relat Res* 162:11–19.

39. Akbarnia, B.A., Torg, J.S., Kirkpartrick, J., et al. 1974. Manifestations of the battered-child syndrome. *J Bone Jt Surg Am* 56:1159–66.

40. Swischuk, L.E. 1969. Spine and spinal cord trauma in the battered child syndrome. *Radiology* 92:733–38.

41. Kleinman, P.K., and Marks, S.C. 1992. Vertebral body fractures in child abuse: Radiologic-histologic correlates. *Invest Radiol* 27:715–22.

42. Kris, V.M., and Kris, T.C. 1996. SCIWORA (spinal cord injury without radiographic abnormality) in infants & children. *Clin Pediatr* 35:119–24.

43. Kleinman, P.K., and Barnes, P.D. 1998. Head trauma. In Kleinman, P.K., *Diagnostic imaging of child abuse*, 2nd ed. Mosby, St. Louis, 285–342.

44. Reece, D.M. 1994. *Child abuse: Medical diagnosis and management*. Lea and Feliger, Philadelphia, 23–50.

45. Billmire, M.E., and Myers, P.A. 1985. Serious head injuries in infants: Accident or abuse? *Pediatrics* 75:340–42.

46. Jain, A.M. 1999. Emergency department evaluation of child abuse. *Emerg Med Clin North Am* 17:575–93.

47. Bilo, R.A.C., Robbin, S.G., and van Rijn, R.R. 2010. *Forensic aspects of paediatric fractures*. Springer, Berlin, 15–45.

48. Harwood-Nash, D.C., Hendrick, E.R., and Hudson, A.R. 1971. The significance of skull fractures in children, a study of 1187 patients. *Radiology* 101:151–56.

49. Helfer, R.E., Slovis, T.L., and Black, M. 1977. Injuries resulting when small children fall out of bed. *Pediatrics* 60:533–35.

50. Nimityongskul, P., and Anderson, L.D. 1987. The likelihood of injuries when children fall out of bed. *J Pediatr Orthop* 7:184–86.

51. Lyons, T.J., and Oates, R.K. 1993. Falling out of bed: A relatively benign occurrence. *Pediatrics* 92:125–27.

52. Hollman, A.S. 1994. Facial trauma. In Carty, H., Brunelle, F., Ringertz, H.G., Shaw, D., and Kendall, B., eds., *Imaging children*. Churchill Livingston, Edinburgh, 1774.

53. Leestma, J.E. 2005. Case analysis of brain-injured admittably shaken infants: 54 cases, 1969–2001. *Am J Forens Med Pathol* 26:199–213.

Credits

Brogdon, B.G., Vogel, H., and McDowell, J.D., eds., *A Radiological Atlas of Abuse, Torture, Terrorism and Inflicted Trauma*, CRC Press, Boca Raton, FL, 2002. Figures 2.4c, 2.10a, b, 2.11b, 2.12, 2.13a, 2.14a–c, 2.15, 2.16, 2.17a, b, 2.18, 2.19, 2.20, 2.24, 2.27a, b, 2.30a, b, 2.31a, 2.32, 2.33d, 2.34a–d, 2.36, 2.37, 2.38, 2.45, 2.48a, b, 2.52, 2.53, 2.54, 2.55.

Citations

Thali, M.J., Viner, M.D., and Brogdon, B.G., eds., *Brogdon's Forensic Radiology*, 2nd ed., CRC Press, Boca Raton, FL, 2011. Figures 2.4c, 2.8, 2.10, 2.17a, b, 2.27a, 2.30, 2.31a, 2.34a–c, 2.37, 2.38, 2.39, 2.43a, 2.46a, 2.48a, b, 2.53, 2.55a, b.

Brogdon, B.G., Vogel, H., and McDowell, J.D., eds., *A Radiological Atlas of Abuse, Torture, Terrorism, and Inflicted Trauma*, CRC Press, Boca Raton, FL, 2002. Figures 2.1b, 2.11a, 2.13, 2.14a, c, 2.15, 2.16, 2.18, 2.19, 2.20, 2.24, 2.25, 2.27, 2.32a–c, 2.33b, 2.35c, 2.36, 2.43b.

Brogdon, B.G., ed., *Forensic Radiology*, CRC Press, Boca Raton, FL, 1998. Figure 2.4d.

Radiological Mimickers of Physical Child Abuse

3

Introduction

Although most of the classic radiological findings in nonaccidental trauma have been described and documented for six decades or more, the diagnosis is not always easy. Some accidental and nonaccidental injuries can be differentiated only in the broad spectrum of context. Other nontraumatic skeletal lesions can closely resemble classic representations of physical abuse. Others may seem rather far-fetched as mimickers of abuse, but when seen as images of individual body parts and without the context of other findings, history, and circumstances, can be confusing. This is particularly true for the relatively untrained and inexperienced individual who first sees the child and has an obligatory legal duty to report suspicion of inflicted trauma.

We will present in this chapter a number of conditions that more or less mimic the radiological manifestations of nonaccidental trauma. For convenience of reference back to the true examples of physical abuse, these conditions are organized similarly to those with apparent metaphyseal lesions, fractures, dislocations, subperiosteal new bone formation, spinal conditions, and findings in the skull. Some of these mimickers, of course, have findings that fit into more than one of these categories.

Metaphyseal Lesions

The most physiologically active area of the growing long bone is the physis or "growth plate" and its borders, the metaphysis and the epiphysis. Since the major processes of chondrification and ossification take place at the metaphyseal margin of the growth plate, it is reasonable to assume that almost any aberration of that process would affect normal growth. We have already seen that it is the weak point for failure from traumatic stress.

The most commonly, and ordinarily the first, mentioned metaphyseal lesions as mimickers of physical abuse are scurvy and rickets. This is somewhat paradoxical since the pathophysiologic bases for these diseases and the changes they produce are entirely antithetical.

Scurvy is derived from a deficiency of vitamin C. It is the classic example of osteoporosis. The osteoid matrix is flawed. The calcification process is not. Osteoporosis is characterized by a sharply defined but thin cortex and diminished bone density. Rickets is the result of abnormal calcium metabolism superimposed on a normal osteoid matrix. This is the classic appearance of osteomalacia with a thickened or normal cortex and a poorly defined corticomedullary junction. The overall quality of the bone density is somewhat variable in appearance, sometimes appearing decreased in density, sometimes increased. The appearance at the end of the growing metaphysis is distinctly different in the two diseases.

Scurvy

Vitamin C deficiency may be a rare entity in modern society; however, the disease continues to be reported in industrialized countries.[1] Ascorbic acid is essential for proper collagen synthesis. Signs of scurvy develop as soon as 1–3 months after inadequate vitamin C intake. Patients often present with dermatologic findings such as petechiae, ecchymoses, and gingival bleeding. However, it is important to note that musculoskeletal manifestations occur in up to 80% of patients with scurvy.[2,3] In the pediatric age group the radiographic findings are directly related to defective osteoid matrix formation and cartilage maturation. These include (from the physis proximally) a thin line of increased density representing the zone of provisional calcification (the white line of Frankel), a marginal spur or beak (Pelken's sign), a line of decreased density (the scurvy line), and another slightly dense irregular metaphyseal margin (Truemmerfeld zone) of increased fragmentation (Figure 3.1). When the secondary ossification center is present, it usually appears somewhat diminished in density, but with a thin, dense encircling margin (Wimberger's sign). These findings are relatively consistent at the growing end of all long bones (Figures 3.2–3.4). Because of the bleeding diathesis, blood collects beneath the periosteum and (because calcium metabolism is normal) calcifies, sometimes to massive proportions (Figures 3.4 and 3.5).

All of these changes may be confused with the classic metaphyseal lesion (CML) and subperiosteal new bone formation seen in nonaccidental trauma and require very careful attention to the total context of the case, including geographic, social, and nutritional considerations.

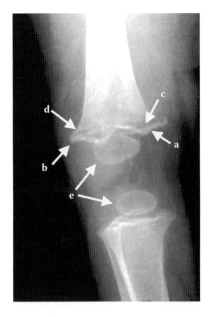

Figure 3.1 Frontal view of the knee of a child with scurvy demonstrating classic radiographic findings: (a) zone of provisional calcification (white line of Frankel), (b) marginal spur or beak (Pelken's sign), (c) scurvy line of decreased density, (d) Truemmerfeld zone of fragmentation, and (e) Wimberger's line of increased density surrounding the secondary ossification center or epiphysis. (From Rich, J., *Forensic Medicine of the Lower Extremity*, Humana Press, Totowa, NJ, 2005, p. 188, Figure 57. With permission of Springer Science+Business Media.)

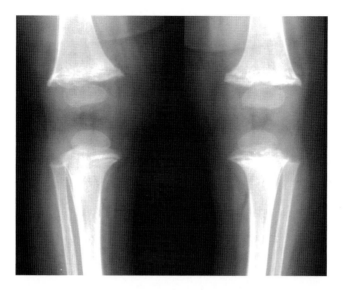

Figure 3.2 Both knees of another child with scurvy demonstrating classic findings at the ends of long bones. Note also the general osteoporosis characterized by overall diminished bone density with thin, sharply defined cortices and distinct differentiation between cortex and medulla.

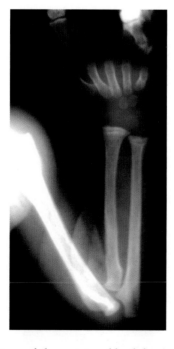

Figure 3.3 Scurvy manifestations of the wrist and both bones of the forearm.

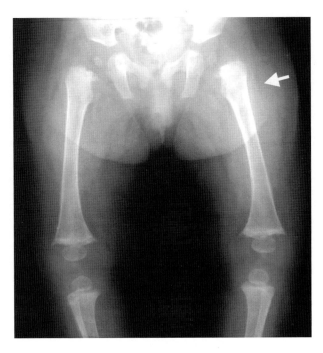

Figure 3.4 Osteoporosis and metaphyseal changes of scurvy at both hips and knees. There is beginning calcification of subperiosteal hemorrhage on the proximal third of the left femur (arrow).

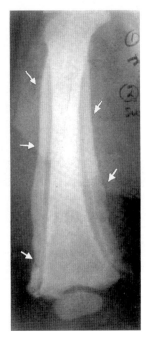

Figure 3.5 Massive subperiosteal new bone formation secondary to hemorrhage enveloping the entire femoral shaft (arrows).

Rickets

By definition, rickets is a disorder of undermineralization of bone in children prior to closure of the growth plates. Vitamin D deficiency is the cause of abnormal bone metabolism. A multitude of disorders can lead to vitamin D deficiency, from the lack of vitamin D intake, to abnormal absorption, to anomalous metabolism. Lack of sunlight and anticonvulsant medications also are directly related to vitamin D deficiency.

Skeletal changes are most marked where rapid growth occurs at the levels of the expected zone of provisional calcification. At first, there is an indistinctness of the distal metaphysis. As the disease progresses there is a fraying of the metaphysis and widening of the growth plate. The shafts of the bone are softened and may bow spontaneously or upon weight bearing. The density of the bone is diminished but is osteomalacic rather than osteoporotic (Figure 3.6). The rachitic rosary, widened, flared rib ends with no opacified zone of provisional calcification, is another classic sign (Figure 3.7). Rickets due to dietary deficiency and insufficient sunlight is relatively uncommon in infants and children in most of the developed countries. In normal situations there is "maternal protection" of the newborn and infant for several months against vitamin deficiency unless the mother is deficient[4] (Figure 3.8). However, rachitic bone changes are at times seen in the premature and intensive care nursery when adequate nutrition, particularly replacement of calcium or phosphorus, cannot be maintained[5,6] (Figure 3.9).

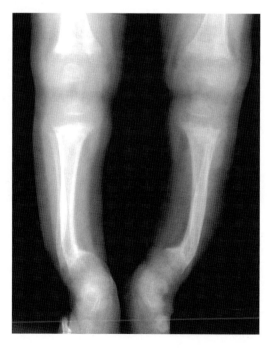

Figure 3.6 Classic manifestations of rickets. The metaphyses are widened with frayed margins. The zone of provisional calcification is diminished or absent. The physis widens because uncalcified osteoid continues to be produced. The bones are soft and bowing may result. The overall quality of the bone is one of osteomalacia, with poor definition between the medulla and the cortex, which is initially widened but may become narrower in time. However, with the diminished cortical calcification it will never be as sharply defined as it is in normal bone or osteoporosis. The epiphyseal centers are poorly mineralized and have no dense peripheral "rind," as in Wimberger's sign of scurvy.

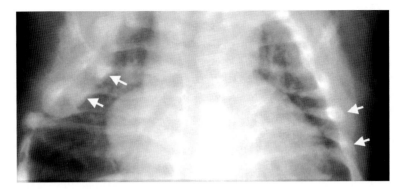

Figure 3.7 Chest radiograph demonstrating classic rachitic rosary, a bulbous expansion of anterior rib ends.

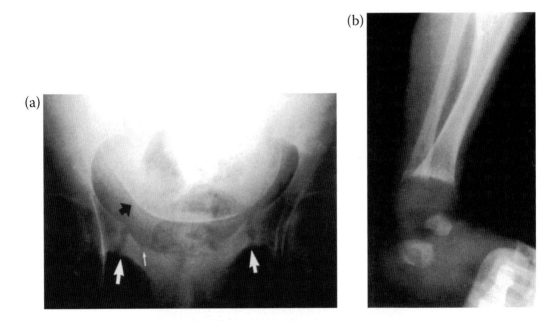

Figure 3.8 (a) This is the lower pelvis of a pregnant Bedouin woman who spends her life totally covered when outside or shielded by an opaque tent when inside. She is at the end of the family "pecking order," after the men and children. She has vitamin D deficiency and severe osteomalacia with insufficiency fractures in the superior pubic rami (white arrows). The skull of a near-term fetus (black arrow) is at the level of the ischial spines. (b) Leg and ankle of the newborn she produced, with classic rachitic findings in the bones.

Similar skeletal findings are seen in children who are vitamin D resistant, and identical changes are found in children and juveniles with renal osteodystrophy. The long-term use of antiepileptic drugs (AEDs) has long been associated with changes in the levels of circulating calcium and calcitropic hormones.[7,8] Specifically, long-term AED treatment is strongly associated with low 25(OH)D levels and consequently hypocalcemia, indicating secondary hyperparathyroidism. Therefore it makes sense that patients with epilepsy who are being treated with AEDs have a greater risk of abnormal mineralization, bone loss, and

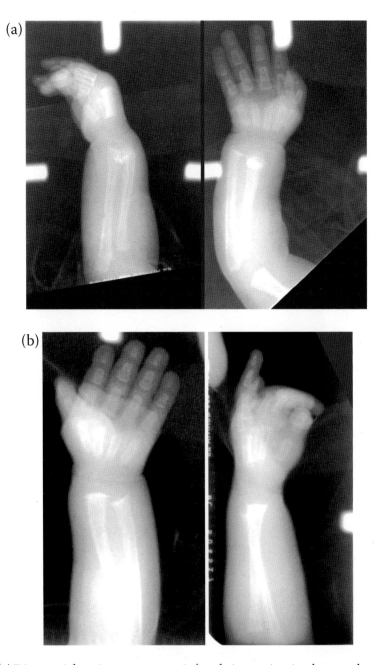

Figure 3.9 (a) Dietary rickets in a premature infant being maintained on total parental nutrition but without adequate calcium or phosphorus replacement. There is a fracture of the distal radius that can occur with normal handling of these very fragile bones. (b) A graduate of the premature nursery with dietary rickets beginning to show signs of an adequate diet. See the early increasing density of the zone of provisional calcification at the ends of the distal metaphyses of the radius and ulna.

fractures. Childhood and adolescence are critical stages for skeletal mineralization. Peak bone mass is not achieved until the second or third decade of life. Children institutionalized for mental deficiencies or seizure disorders are particularly at risk for overdose. Severe rachitic changes may be seen, and the softened bones are prone to bowing and fracture with ordinary handling or restraint (Figure 3.10).

With healing, rickets may appear even more suspicious for abuse because the zone of provisional calcification will begin to increase in density, distal to the noncalcified osteoid, thus simulating a metaphyseal fracture (Figure 3.11). With vitamin therapy, subperiosteal bleeding and calluses will begin to calcify (Figure 3.12).

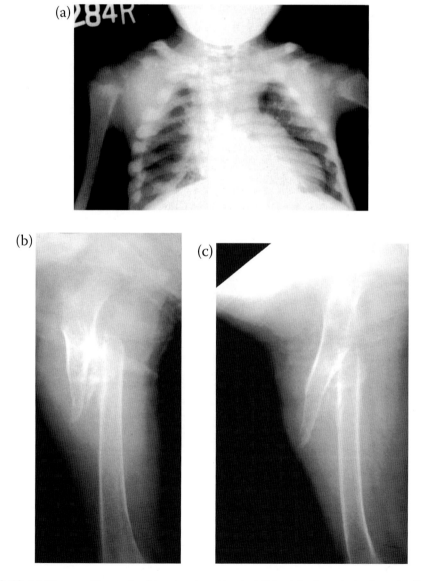

Figure 3.10 (a) Chest radiograph of institutionalized child with chronic hydantoin (Dilantin) overdose. Florid rachitic changes are seen at the humeral metaphyses and a classic rachitic rosary at rib ends. (b, c) Oblique, displaced, overriding fracture of the fragile, osteomalacic femoral shaft incurred during normal handling.

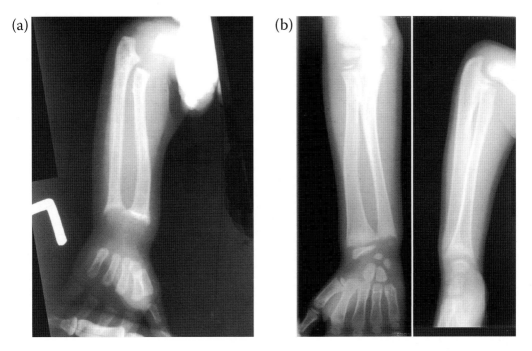

Figure 3.11 (a) Infant under treatment for rickets. Note the increasing but irregular density in the zone of proximal calcification with cupping and marginal spurs, which might be confused with a CML. However, the bones still have a malacic pattern. (b) Slightly older child under treatment. Note the thickness of the uncalcified physis is approaching normal, as is the corticomedullary distinction.

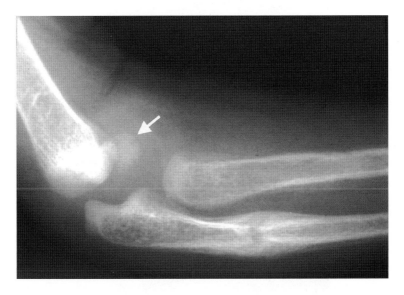

Figure 3.12 Rachitic institutionalized child from hydantoin overdose after withdrawal and treatment. Note calcification of periarticular hemorrhage (arrow) and of callus at the healing fracture site.

Menkes Disease (Kinky-Hair Syndrome)

A neurodegenerative disorder first described in 1962, Menkes disease is an x-linked recessive inherited disease of copper metabolism.[9] Deficiency of copper leads to various neurologic, hematologic, dermatologic, and musculoskeletal abnormalities. In Menkes disease, copper deficiency is secondary to faulty intestinal copper absorption. Laboratory evaluation of copper and ceruloplasmin is possible; however, these values are often low in normal newborns for the first 2–3 weeks of life. Hair abnormalities are the best-known trait of Menkes (Figures 3.13 and 3.14). Patients also display characteristic facies, various degrees of mental retardation, bladder diverticulae, and skin and joint laxity.[10]

Radiographic findings include diaphyseal periosteal reaction and metaphyseal spurring (Figures 3.15 and 3.16) suggestive of trauma.[11] Long-bone and rib fractures secondary to generalized osteoporosis are not uncommon, again suggestive of abusive trauma.[12] Anterior flaring of the ribs and periostitis of the clavicles have been reported. The skull may be normal in size at birth, but slowing of the growth rate ensues. Wormian bones are common (Figure 3.17). Occipital horns are sometimes encountered, and when present, these exostoses are diagnostic of a milder form of the disease occipital horn syndrome.[13] Subsequent CT and MRI investigation demonstrate cerebral atrophy, ventricular enlargement, and extra-axial collections of fluid that may contain blood[14,15] (Figure 3.18).

Congenital Syphilis

Syphilis nowadays is a relatively rare, preventable, and treatable disease. The causal mechanism of congenital syphilis is transplacental spread of treponema pallidum (syphilis) from an infected mother to her fetus. The incidence of the disease was substantially reduced

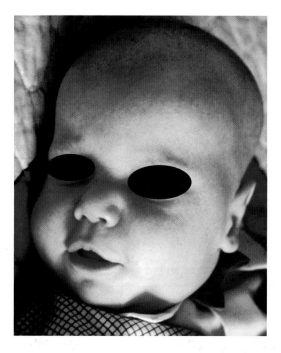

Figure 3.13 Male infant with Menkes disease. The wiry copperish hair on head and eyebrows is the obvious origin of the synonym: kinky-hair syndrome.

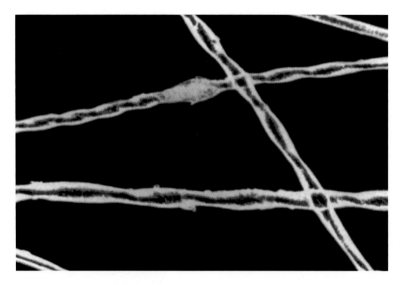

Figure 3.14 Low-power microscopy reveals the peculiar morphology of the hair, which gives the condition its name.

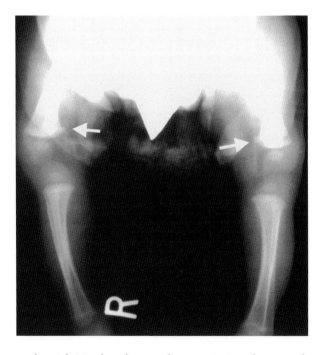

Figure 3.15 Infant male with Menkes disease demonstrating the metaphyseal beaking at the knee and generalized osteoporosis.

after World War II by penicillin treatment. Unfortunately there has been a resurgence of the disease worldwide in recent decades. Congenital syphilis is uncommon, but unfortunately, not a rarity in children's hospitals and large general hospitals today.

Clinically, newborns may exhibit failure to thrive, fever, irritability, rashes, saddle nose deformities, hepatosplenomegaly, and rashes on the palms of the hands and the soles of

(a)   (b)

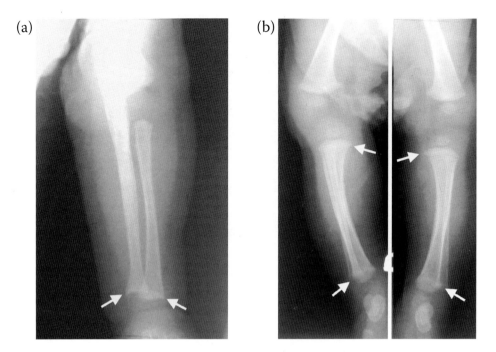

Figure 3.16 A slightly older male with Menkes disease showing osteoporosis of long bones and metaphyseal beaking at (a) the wrist and (b) the knees and ankles.

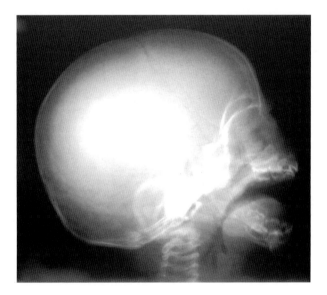

Figure 3.17 Lateral view of the skull with wormian bones in the lambdoid suture but no occipital horn. Menkes disease.

the feet. Older children may exhibit abnormally notched teeth (referred to as Hutchinson teeth), blindness, and impaired hearing/deafness. Approximately 25% of children with congenital syphilis will have bony manifestations that can simulate nonaccidental trauma.[16] The archetypal descriptions of congenital syphilis with radiographic correlations were made in the 1930s.[17–19] Lucent transverse metaphyseal bands, metaphyseal erosions, and

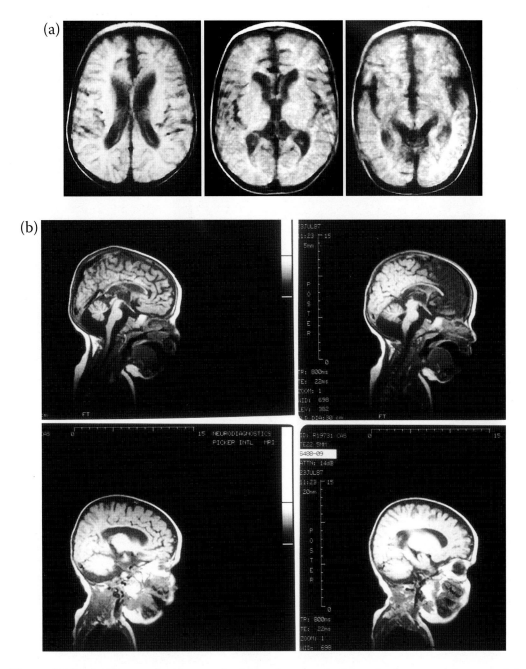

Figure 3.18 (a) CT scan showing cerebral atrophy, ventricular enlargement, and extra-axial fluid collections. (b) Sagittal MRI showing similar findings. Menkes disease.

irregular lytic defects are common (Figure 3.19). Periosteal reactions and pathologic fractures are also well-known responses to syphilitic osteomyelitis. Fractures commonly occur through the metaphyses due to damage from syphilitic gummatous granulation tissue[20] (Figure 3.20). Skeletal changes most often involve the tibia, femur, and humerus. Bowing of long bones, such as saber shin, is a typical feature in older victims. Congenital syphilis seen originally as a skeletal lesion can easily be mistaken for child abuse.[21]

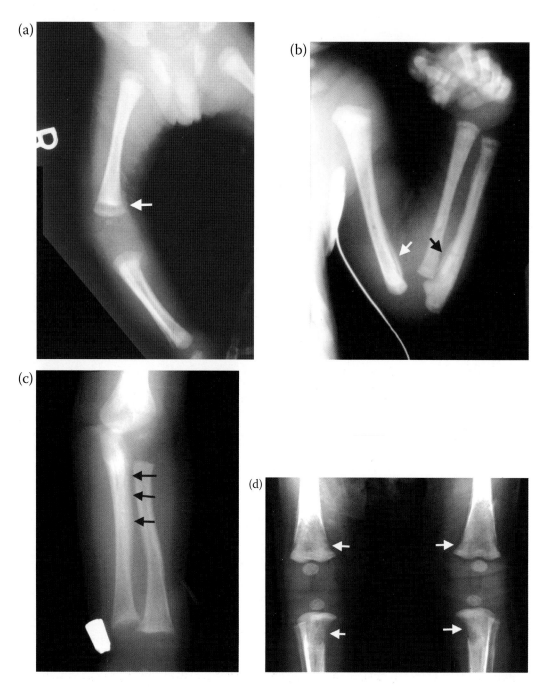

Figure 3.19 (a, b) Newborn with congenital syphilis. Note the bands of diminished density across the distal metaphyses of the femur, both ends of the tibia, the proximal humerus, and distal humerus, radius, and ulna (arrows). There is early periostitis on the distal humerus and proximal ulna (arrows). (c) Early periostitis along the proximal ulna in congenital syphilis; the bones are neither osteoporotic nor malacic. (d) Infant with large gummatous destructive area in the metaphyses around the knees (arrows) and associated periostitis at the junction of the diaphysis and metaphysis of the femora.

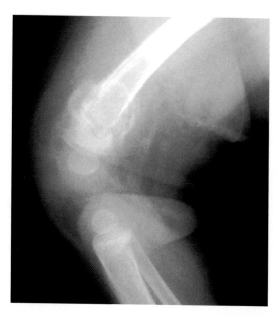

Figure 3.20 Fracture through syphilitic osteomyelitis in the metaphysis of the distal femur with abundant periosteal reaction.

Intrauterine Infection

Other intrauterine congenital infections may cause confusion with nonaccidental trauma.

Rubella (German Measles)

Infection with rubella is a serious affectation of women who become pregnant while their disease is active. The virus is capable of transuterine infection of the fetus with serious, sometimes fatal, results.

The radiological manifestations are present at birth of the infected fetus, including affectations of the musculoskeletal system. The disease is a viral osteomyelitis, although pathological/histological findings of osteomyelitis are usually absent.

The fetal long bones display *no* periosteal reaction. The metaphyses of long bones, particularly those at the knee, are most often clearly affected. The lack of normal modeling of the long bones results in widened metaphyseal ends. The long shaft is of increased radioopacity. The flared metaphyses show alternating longitudinal striae of dense and lucent bands. Williams and Carey[22] aptly compared the appearance of the long bones and their metaphyses to a stalk of celery (Figure 3.21). A significant negative finding is that there is *no* accompanying periostitis. Somewhat similar changes can result from other intrauterine viral infections of the fetus.

Fetal Cytomegalovirus Infection

Fetal cytomegalovirus infection is the most commonly observed at this time. There are rubella-like bone changes, but there tend to be more ovoid lucencies interspersed in the longitudinal striations. The metaphyseal ends may become serrated, and Graham and associates[23] suggested that these resembled "bitten celery" (Figure 3.22).

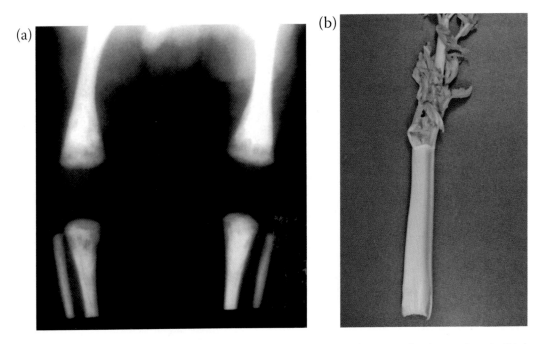

Figure 3.21 (a) Classic appearance of intrauterine rubella infection. The femoral and tibial metaphyses at the knee are poorly modeled and flared. The distal diaphyses and metaphyses are increased in density. The ends of the metaphyses are striated with longitudinal lucent bands resembling (b) a celery stalk.

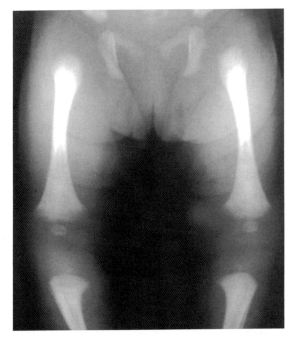

Figure 3.22 Congenital cytomegalic viral infection with rubella-like changes. The longitudinal lucent striations are partially interrupted by ovoid lucencies. The serrated ends of the metaphyseal involvement are said to resemble bitten celery.

Metaphyseal Chondrodysplasias

Schmid Type

There is a spectrum of abnormalities of the physis and metaphysis of immature long bones that fall under the umbrella of metaphyseal chondrodysplasias. Among these separate clinical entities, Schmid type is the most common and Jansen type is the most severe.[24] We focus first on the Schmid type, which was described by Schmid in 1949.[25] A mutation on chromosome 6 is responsible for the defective type X collagen.[26]

Skeletal abnormalities of Schmid-type chondrodysplasia are most striking in the distal metaphyses of long bones, especially the femur. The metaphyses are flared and irregular with fragmentation. The femoral epiphyses are enlarged and there is coxa vara deformity of the hips (Figure 3.23). Rib abnormalities similar to ricketic changes can be seen. However, the spine is often normal. Given these findings, Schmid-type chondrodysplasia has been confused with nonaccidental trauma as well as rickets. Jansen type, McKusick type, and Schwachman type are more rare, more severe, and involve other sites and organs. Even so, the radiograph of an isolated affected joint with metaphyseal alteration may cause confusion[27] (Figure 3.24).

Leukemia

Leukemia is the most common childhood malignancy. The most common type of childhood leukemia is acute lymphoblastic leukemia (ALL). Most children present with musculoskeletal pain secondary to the massive proliferation of the hematopoietic elements within the medullary cavities, which occurs most frequently in the vertebral bodies and long bones.[28] Pain may be out of proportion to clinical findings.[29] The peak incidence is in children aged 2–5 years. It has been reported that bone involvement serves as a negative prognostic factor.[30]

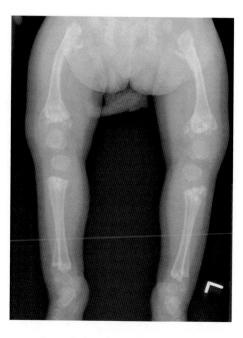

Figure 3.23 Schmid-type metaphyseal chondrodysplasia. Flared metaphyses at the distal femur, and to a lesser degree at the proximal tibia with irregularity and fragmentation; may be confused with nonaccidental trauma. The femurs appear bowed and there is coxa vara deformity at the hips.

The most common radiographic findings associated with leukemia include metaphyseal bands, lytic lesions, sclerotic lesions, and periosteal reactions.[31] The narrow radiolucent metaphyseal bands are referred to as leukemic lines. As with any bone abnormality, pathologic fractures may be the presenting sign. Classic leukemic lines are most often seen at the knee, and even though the age is inconsistent, may be confused with the classic CML (Figures 3.25 and 3.26).

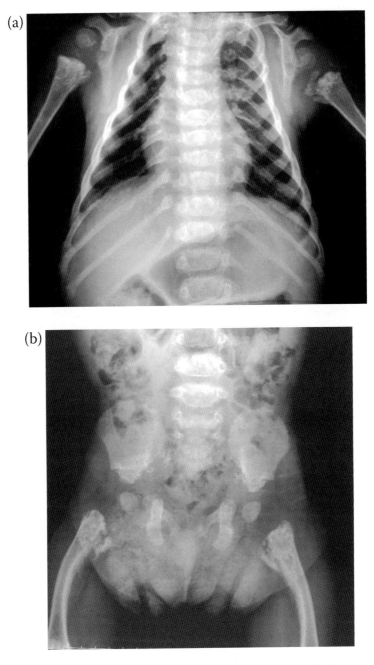

Figure 3.24 Jansen-type variation is more florid. (a) Chest radiograph showing metaphyseal changes at the proximal humeri. (b) Hips.

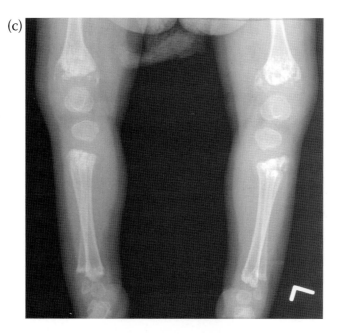

Figure 3.24 (Continued) Jansen-type variation is more florid. (c) Knees. Findings, particularly at the distal femora, could be confused with corner fractures.

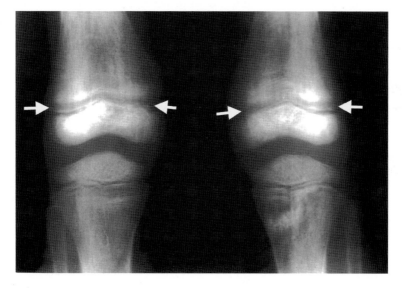

Figure 3.25 Acute lymphoblastic leukemia in an older child. The line of rarefaction just below the zone of proximal calcification (arrows) simulates the CML, but in the wrong age group.

Meningococcemia

Children who survive acute meningococcemia associated with disseminated intravascular coagulation are left with long-term sequellae, especially as a result of the vascular injuries.[32] The skeleton is a prime target. Growth plates subject to ischemic damage display substantial alterations in both epiphyses and metaphyses that persist for years and may be confused with physical trauma if examined singularly and without the pertinent past

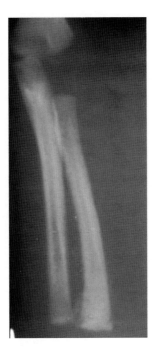

Figure 3.26 Periosteal elevation and calcification in a child with a bleeding diathesis from acute leukemia. Periosteal reaction from bleeding and periosteal elevation is common but a nonspecific finding for many conditions, including nonaccidental trauma. Focal areas of destruction of cortical or medullary bone are seen, but not commonly.

history (Figure 3.27). The diaphyses show subperiosteal new bone formation in the acute stage of the disease, but ordinarily show complete recovery.

Little Leaguer's Shoulder

This injury, self-inflicted by the throwing action, is a Salter-Harris epiphyseal fracture of either type 1 or type 2 (Figure 3.28). It is identical in appearance to similar injuries resulting from nonaccidental trauma (compare with Figure 2.13). Of course, Little Leaguer's shoulder is seen in young adolescents and the history is all-important. It is less common and less well known than Little Leaguer's elbow, and hence less often immediately diagnosed.[33,34] We have seen a young pitcher in whom the nature of the radiographic finding was unrecognized by his father, a radiologist.

Hypophosphatasia

A rare inheritable metabolic disorder of the skeleton, the birth prevalence of hypophosphatasia is 1/100,000. It is a complex disorder with variable presentations (Figure 3.29). Six main types are described in the literature: lethal perinatal, infantile, childhood, adult, odontohypophosphatasia, and an extremely rare benign prenatal form with a better prognosis than the other prenatal form. The subtypes may overlap, and inheritance may be autosomal recessive or dominant with variable expressivity.

(a) (b) (c)

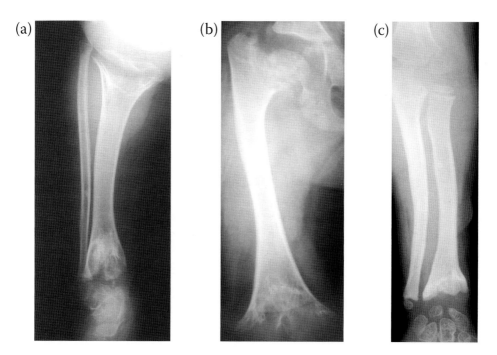

Figure 3.27 (a) Widening, cupping, fraying, and abnormal areas of sclerosis and lucency in the tibial metaphyses of a child after meningococcemia. (b) The femur shows alteration of the head and neck with varus deformity. The diaphysis is thickened and dense from periostitis. Changes in the distal metaphysis are similar to those in the tibia. (c) Similar changes at the wrist and elbow. The diaphyses are still thickened and dense from periosteal reaction, which should eventually remodel to essentially normal appearance.

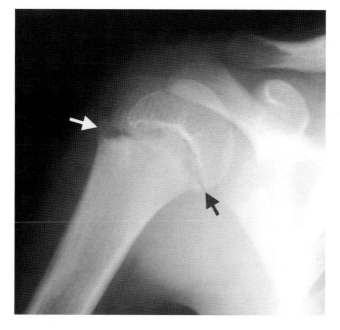

Figure 3.28 Classic appearance of Little Leaguer's shoulder, a Salter-Harris type 1 or 2 fracture of the proximal humeral epiphysis of the throwing arm (arrows).

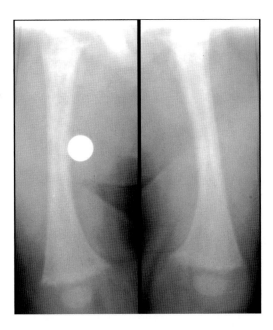

Figure 3.29 Hypophosphatasia. Note the osteomalacic bony pattern, the widened metaphyses with mottled and frayed ends, and unilaminar periosteal reaction.

The lethal perinatal form is discovered in utero with markedly impaired mineralization. Pathognomonic skin-covered osteochondral spurs protrude from the forearms and legs.[35] Most infants cannot survive because of significant respiratory compromise due to hypoplastic lungs and rachitic deformities of the chest.

The prenatal benign form has spontaneous improvement of the skeletal defects.[36] Patients may present with limb shortening and bowing.

Children with the infantile form may appear normal at birth. Clinical signs often appear within the first 6 months, and these children often suffer from respiratory difficulty secondary to rachitic deformities of the chest. Radiographs typically show extensive undermineralization and rachitic changes in bones. Premature craniosynostosis is also common and may result in increased intracranial pressure.[37] These children may have failure to thrive, hypercalcemia, short stature, and premature loss of deciduous teeth.

The childhood form exhibits short stature, abnormal gait, enlarged joints, and a dolichocephalic skull. These patients may also have abnormal dentition, intracranial hypertension, failure to thrive, and focal bony defects near the ends of long bones, and a history of bone pain and fractures.[38]

Stippled Epiphyses

This is a rare disorder characterized by multiple discrete punctate calcifications in the expected location of the epiphyses but often before their time of expected ossification. There are many synonyms: chondrodystrophia calcificans congenita, dysplasia epiphysealis punctata, chondroangiopathia calcarea seu punctata, and epiphyseal dysplasia punticularis. The condition is present at birth. Once known, it is easily demonstrated and diagnosed radiographically. Common areas of involvement are the hips, knees, shoulders, wrists, vertebrae, pelvis, and rib ends (Figures 3.30 and 3.31). Even the hyoid bone was involved in one case reported.[39]

There may be other associated abnormalities: saddle nose, monomelic shortening and bowing, particularly of the humeri and femora, widening of metaphyses, microcephal, cleft palate, cardiac defects (usually atrial septal defect), and cataracts, among others.

With maturation the punctuate densities disappear peripherally and central portions of the epiphyses develop relatively normally (Figure 3.32). Some deformity may persist, but a completely normal-appearing epiphysis may ensue. It is in the latter stages of maturation that the changes in the secondary ossification center, associated with the metaphyseal widening, could cause confusion if an isolated joint is imaged without observation of the child or knowledge of his or her history (see also under "The Spine").

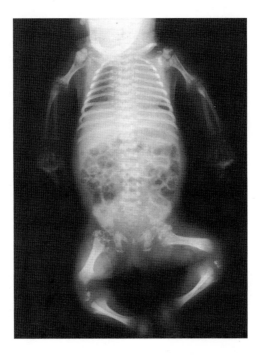

Figure 3.30 "Babygram" of a newborn with stippled epiphyses at many joints.

(a)

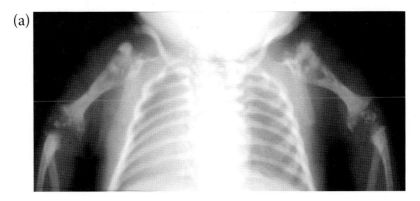

Figure 3.31 (a) Punctate calcification in the expected location of secondary ossification centers at the shoulder and elbow in a newborn.

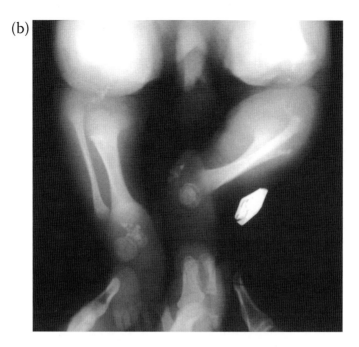

Figure 3.31 (*Continued*) (b) Same infant with stippling of knee epiphyses. Note also the shortening and slight bowing of long bones and the widened metaphyseal ends.

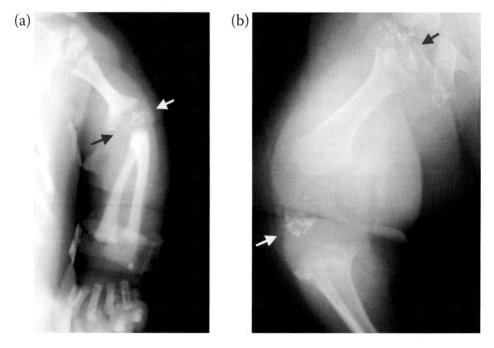

Figure 3.32 Another infant with more dense coalescent stippling at (a) the shoulder and elbows and (b) the knee. (An identification bracelet creates an artifact over the wrist.)

Fractures and Bowing

The difficulty in determining whether fractures in infants and children are accidental or nonaccidental has been discussed earlier. The differentiation often depends on the total context since the resultant radiological appearance can be identical. We present here some lesions that could be, or have been, confused with inflicted trauma, but in which careful examination of the appearance or circumstances of the injury should alleviate suspicion.

Perinatal Fractures/Birth Injuries

The perinatal period extends from the 20th to the 29th week of gestation to 1–4 weeks after birth. Many of these injuries will occur during delivery or in the nursery, where they will be appreciated almost immediately. Even if diagnosis is delayed, the circumstance will be exculpatory. Some fractures will not be discovered until after the baby has been taken home, and here context becomes increasingly important and helpful.[40,41]

Intrapartum clavicular fractures are particularly likely to escape notice. They may be glimpsed unexpectedly on the margin of a chest radiograph obtained for some other indication, or the complex curves of the normal clavicle that is ill-positioned may simulate a healed fracture deformity (Figure 3.33). A soft tissue bump over a nonappositional fracture or the subsequent callus mass may attract attention, often during the first well-baby checkup (Figure 3.34). Calluses can form in the neonate within 7 days, so a fracture with no calluses 10 days postpartum arouses suspicion. Past that interval, the maturity of the callus must be assessed, but timing of the duration of fractures by this method is fraught with uncertainty. Therefore other factors must be considered since inflicted trauma in the neonatal period is not uncommon. While the clavicle is not a common target for abuse or

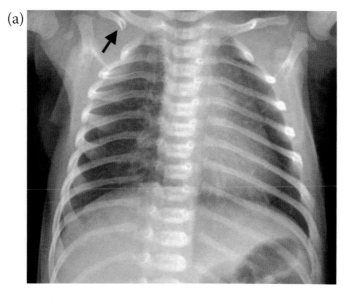

(a)

Figure 3.33 (a) Old displaced fracture of the clavicle seen on the margin of a chest radiograph obtained for another purpose.

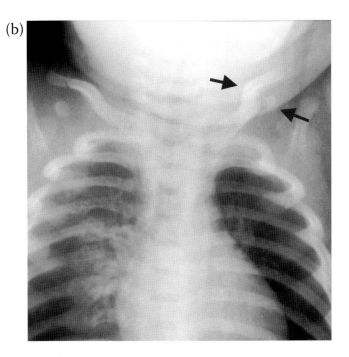

Figure 3.33 (*Continued*) (b) The double-curved configuration of the normal clavicle may appear deformed, thickened, and foreshortened due to faulty positioning (arrows). This may simulate a healed fracture to the experienced viewer.

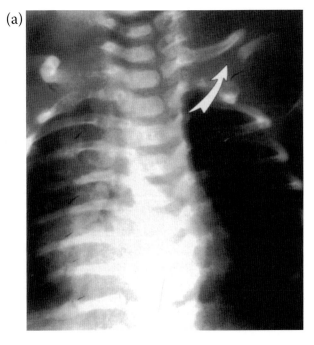

Figure 3.34 (a) Overriding, nonoppositional fracture of the clavicle occurring in childbirth but not diagnosed at the time, resulting in non-union and palpable deformity.

(b)

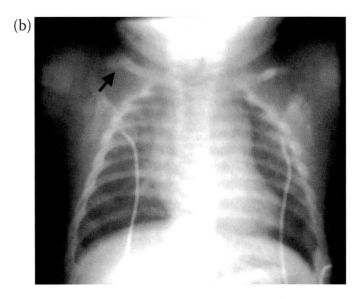

Figure 3.34 (*Continued*) (b) Clavicular fracture occurring at childbirth (arrow) but not appreciated until the callus mass attracted attention during a routine well-baby checkup.

(a)   (b)

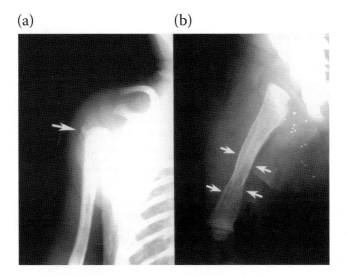

Figure 3.35 Fractures sustained during an intrauterine version procedure for a transverse lie. (a) Proximal humeral metaphysis. (b) Femoral shaft. (The white dots are film artifacts.) These radiographs were obtained a few days postpartum—hence the periosteal new bone at both sites.

trauma, the other two most common sites for birth trauma—the femur and humerus—certainly are.[42] Birth fractures can occur in association with cesarean section as well as during vaginal delivery and forceps or vacuum extraction.[43,44] Accidental injury to the skull during childbirth is covered later in this chapter.

Fetal version, usually to correct a transverse lie, is uncommon in modern obstetrical practice with the increasing incidence of cesarean section. External or bimanual version (with one hand external and the other in the birth canal/uterus) may still be found in more primitive delivery situations. Fractures of extremities may be sustained in the process (Figure 3.35).

Handling or "Nursing" Fractures

Accidental fractures of long bones may occur in the course of normal handling of infants in the hospital nursery setting, in long-term care facilities, as a result of physiotherapy, during the click test for hip dislocation, as a complication of intraosseous vascular access needle placement (the needle track itself can mimic a fracture), and even during routine home care. The context of the situation and plausibility of the history is all important in order to distinguish these unfortunate episodes from nonaccidental trauma.[45–49]

These injuries are more likely in bones weakened by prematurity/immaturity, dietary deficiency, disease, or medication. The extremities are used as convenient and sometimes necessary handles when moving, repositioning, examining, or restraining the infant or child. The humerus and femur are the most convenient handles and most likely sites of these fractures (Figure 3.36). We also have seen fractures just above the ankles from the usual one-handed grip to lift a baby for perineal care or diaper changing. (We have seen similar long-bone handling fractures in elder patients with marked osteoporosis.[50])

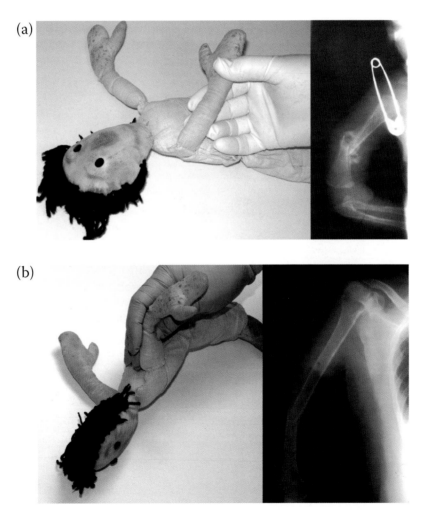

(a)

(b)

Figure 3.36 Fractures of the humerus or femur can be incurred by simply lifting (a) or turning (b) a fragile infant in the nursery.

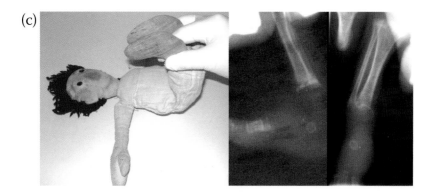

Figure 3.36 (*Continued*) Fractures just above the ankles (c) can be incurred by simply lifting the infant for a diaper change.

Osteogenesis Imperfecta (OI)

Osteogenesis imperfecta is the prototypical example of a metabolic process simulating nonaccidental trauma. Once the darling of defense attorneys in child abuse cases, it now is widely known, usually diagnosed without confusion, and in difficult cases can be positively confirmed by culturing fibroblasts or by genetic testing. OI is a heterogeneous group of genetic disorders that results in abnormal type I collagen. The incidence rate of osteogenesis imperfecta is approximately 1 in 10,000, or 0.01%.[51] There is a wide spectrum of clinical and radiological presentations. Four main subtypes of OI have been described. All demonstrate multiple osseous fractures, usually resulting from minimal trauma.[52]

Type I OI is most common and is a dominantly inherited, generalized connective tissue disorder characterized mainly by bone fragility and blue sclerae. The collagen structure is normal, but the amount is less than normal. Osseous deformities are least severe in type I disease. Two thirds of patients develop dentinogenesis imperfecta with yellow or brown discoloration of the teeth, enamel fractures of the frontal incisors, and x-ray evidence of bell-shaped crowns and wide pulp chambers.[53] Hearing impairment occurs secondary to otosclerosis in up to 50% of patients. Other classic features include easily bruised skin, moderate joint hypermobility, and kyphoscoliosis. This is the type that may be confused with physical abuse.

Type II OI typically presents with severe fractures in utero. Collagen is improperly formed. At birth, there is severe limb shortening, enlarged calvarium with wormian bones, blue sclerae, and generalized skeletal dysplasia. Death generally occurs in the early prenatal period or infancy. Therefore it is unlikely to be confused with nonaccidental trauma. Furthermore, family history is usually positive in types I and II.

Type III is similar to, but less severe than, type II. There is often severe bowing and shortening of the limbs, normal to light blue sclerae, and fractures at birth are common. Type III is inherited in an autosomal recessive pattern; therefore family history is often negative.

Type IV, fortunately, is extremely rare since it can be confused with abuse. The bone fractures easily and patients generally have a white sclerae.

The radiographic findings can vary according to the severity of the disease. Multiple irregular bones within the cranial sutures, wormian bones, are common but not specific for OI. Softening of the cranial base can lead to basilar impression, that is, migration of C1 and C2 upward into the skull base, invaginating the foramen magnum.

Figure 3.37 Osteogenesis imperfecta (OI): Osteoporotic leg bones with fresh transverse fracture of the tibia and rotary displacement of the thin, gracile fibula.

The appendicular skeleton is osteoporotic (Figure 3.37). Diaphyseal fractures often are angulated and heal with abundant or excessive calluses (Figure 3.38). Remodeling leads to deformed, long, gracile long bones (Figure 3.39).

Spinal abnormalities include collapse and flattening of vertebral bodies (platyspondylitis) and scoliosis. Invagination of the femoral heads into the acetabula produces protrusio acetabuli, sometimes known as Otto pelvis or arthrokatadysis (Figure 3.40).

Temporary Brittle Bone Disease (TBBD)

In 1993 Paterson and co-workers in Dundee[54] proposed the concept of brittle bone disease based on a series of 39 infants presenting with unexplained fractures in the first year of life. They have since produced a number of articles and oral presentations supportive of a "new" entity.[54-57]

Arguments that TBBD is a real entity and not misdiagnosed nonaccidental trauma include: (1) the patient has both clinical and radiological findings similar to OI, (2) there is a substantial discrepancy between radiological evidence of fractures and clinical evidence of trauma, (3) the syndrome occurs in situations where nonaccidental trauma can be confidently excluded, and (4) in over 70 patients returned to parental care there has been no further evidence of abuse.[58]

Paterson's group attributes the findings to temporary collagen abnormality related to some elemental deficiency (e.g., copper) or transient estrogenesis imperfecta. Osteopenia associated with decreased fetal movement also has been suggested as an etiological culprit.[54]

The entity has not been generally accepted, as evidenced by a plethora of dissenting articles, editorials, and opinions.[59,60] Paterson's series has been criticized for scientific and statistical deficiencies. The General Medical Council of Great Britain struck off Paterson as an expert

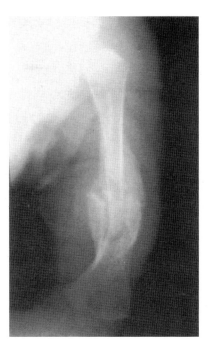

Figure 3.38 Angulated transverse fracture of the humerus with hyperabundant callus typical of OI.

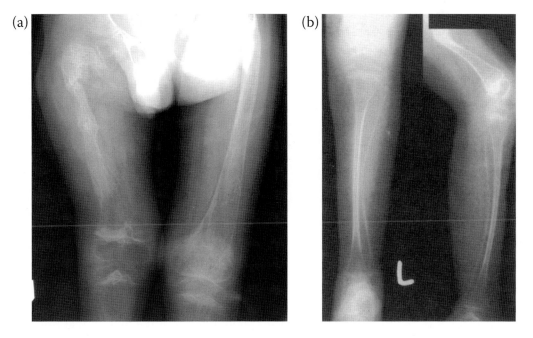

Figure 3.39 (a) Deformed, angulated healed, and healing fractures of the femur in OI. (b) Extremely gracile remodeled leg bones with residual bowing.

(c)

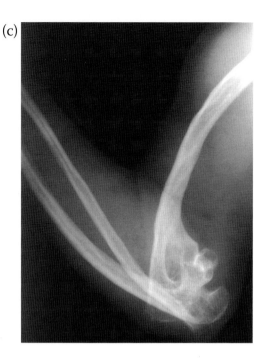

Figure 3.39 (*Continued*) (c) Bowed, gracile, subluxated bones about the elbow following repeated fractures and remodeling from OI.

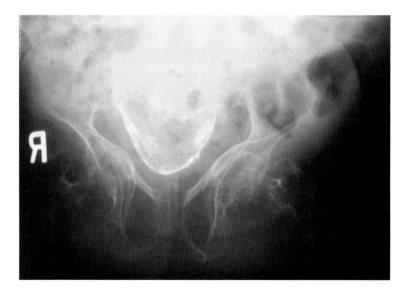

Figure 3.40 Pelvis of a 54-year-old man with pelvic deformation, including protrusio acetabulae from longstanding OI. The large density in the pelvis is a huge calcified fecalith.

witness in cases in Great Britain and the United States for failing to follow his own diagnostic criteria consistently and for ignoring bruising that was inconsistent with his views.[61,62]

We do not recommend this diagnosis at present but repeat the caution that fractures and other traumatic lesions in infants and children must be considered in context. Family and nutritional history may indicate the necessity for appropriate biochemical testing.

Bowing Deformities

Neurofibromatosis

Neurofibromatosis is a multisystemic disease with two main subtypes. Type 1 neurofibromatosis (NF1) is known as von Recklinghausen's disease after the man who first associated the origin of the disorder to tumors arising from cells of the nerve sheaths in 1882.[63] The inheritance pattern is autosomal dominant and affects 1 in 4,000 individuals. It is one of the most common dominantly inherited genetic disorders in humans.[64,65] Common nonmusculoskeletal manifestations include café-au-lait spots, freckling in the axillary and inguinal regions, Lisch nodules, and plexiform neuromas.

NF1 is associated with many skeletal abnormalities, including generalized diminished bone density and increased fracture risk, sphenoid wing dysplasia, optic neuromas with widening of the optic foramena, eighth nerve neuroma with destruction of the petrous ridge apex, scoliosis of the spine, posterior scalloping of vertebral bodies from neuromas of spinal nerves, lateral thoracic meningoceles, anterolateral bowing (kyphoscoliosis) of the tibia progressing to pseudarthrosis, and focal gigantism. Endosteal scalloping and periosteal thickening are seen in the diaphyses of long bones. Cutaneous neurofibromas may appear on roentgenographs as rounded focal areas of increased density with sharp margins because they interface with environmental "outside" air.[66]

Holt points out that the anterolateral bowing is virtually pathognomonic of the disease. The tibia invariably is longer than the fibula, which may or may not be bowed.[66] The case we illustrate is somewhat unusual in that the pseudarthrosis developed in the fibula rather than the tibia (Figure 3.41).

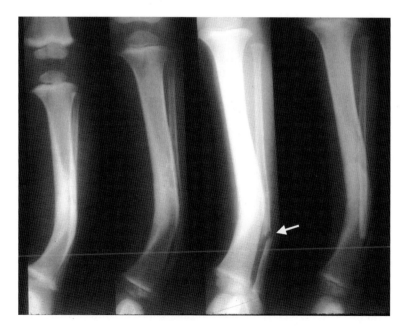

Figure 3.41 Neurofibromatosis type 1. Progression of kyphoscoliosis of the tibia leading, in this instance, to pseudarthrosis of the fibula rather than the tibia, as is the usual case. (From Rich, J., *Forensic Medicine of the Lower Extremity*, Humana Press, Totowa, NJ, 2005, p. 145, Figure 20. With permission of Springer Science+Business Media.)

Other Causes of Bowing Deformity

Multiple etiologies of lower extremity bowing are common in children. We have already discussed osteogenesis imperfecta and neurofibromatosis as sources of bowing deformity. Other causes to recognize, within the scope of this discussion, include congenital bowing, developmental bowing, Blount disease (tibia vara), and Ellis-van Creveld disease (chondroectodermal dysplasia).[67]

Congenital Bowing

Congenital bowing is uncommon and is linked to abnormal uterine position. Most often the tibia bows posteriorly and medially (the opposite of kyphoscoliosis of the tibia in neurofibromatosis). Prognosis is favorable with remodeling during growth, although there may be residual leg-length discrepancy.

Developmental "Physiologic" Bowing

Developmental "physiologic" bowing manifests as varus angulation of the knee with mild enlargement and depression of the proximal tibia metaphyses posteromedially. There should not be any fragmentation of the growth plate, referred to as metaphyseal beaking. This is commonly seen in children who ambulate at an early age and is generally self-correcting by 2 years of age.

Tibia vara (Blount Disease)

Tibia vara (Blount disease) is a bowing deformity that is most likely secondary to abnormal mechanical stress on the posteromedial proximal tibia physis, causing growth suppression. Again, the major deformity is varus angulation at the knee. Three types are recognized, with the infantile type being most common. Children at increased risk are those who walk early, those who are obese, or those who are of African American descent. Unlike the physiologic variety, there is a depression and irregularity or fragmentation of the metaphysis with metaphyseal beaking. There is abrupt lateral bending of the medial cortex wall of the proximal tibial metaphasis and, in the older child, deformity and retarded development of the ipsilateral epiphyseal plateau[68] (Figure 3.42). Blount disease is usually unilateral, while developmental bowing is classically symmetrical.

Ellis-van Creveld Syndrome (Chondroectodermal Dysplasia)

Chondroectodermal dysplasia is an autosomal recessive disorder with polydactyly, syndactyly, ectodermal dysplasia, congenital heart disease, narrowed thoracic cavity, and dwarfism. Delayed and abnormal eruption of teeth may be evident at birth. One-third of those affected expire in the neonatal period, most likely secondary to concomitant cardiac and respiratory compromise. The syndrome was first described in 1940 by R. Ellis and S. van Creveld.[69] The EvC gene is found on the short arm of chromosome 4. Although the exact prevalence is unknown, Ellis-van Creveld syndrome is more common among the Amish population, specifically a subset in Pennsylvania.[70,71]

The most common characteristics of skeletal findings include polydactyly and syndactyly of the hands and feet as well as carpal fusion and acromesomelic upper and lower extremities. Hypoplasia of the lateral proximal tibial epiphysis causes a pronounced genu valgum deformity of the knee, which has been referred to as reverse Blount's deformity.[70] Metaphyseal irregularity in the setting of this clinical picture should not be mistaken for fracture (Figures 3.43 and 3.44).

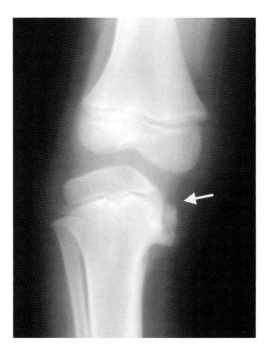

Figure 3.42 Blount disease (tibia vara) with almost vertical orientation of the deformed and deficient epiphyseal plateau, and bending and beaking of the medial aspect of the proximal tibial metaphysis.

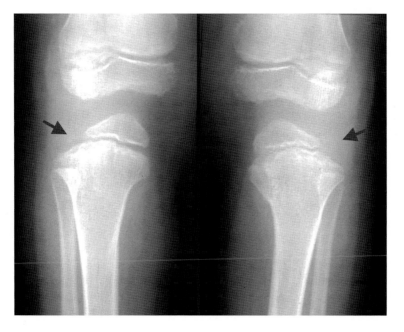

Figure 3.43 "Reverse Blount disease" affecting the lateral components of the proximal tibial plateau in this child with chondroectodermal dysplasia (Ellis-van Creveld disease).

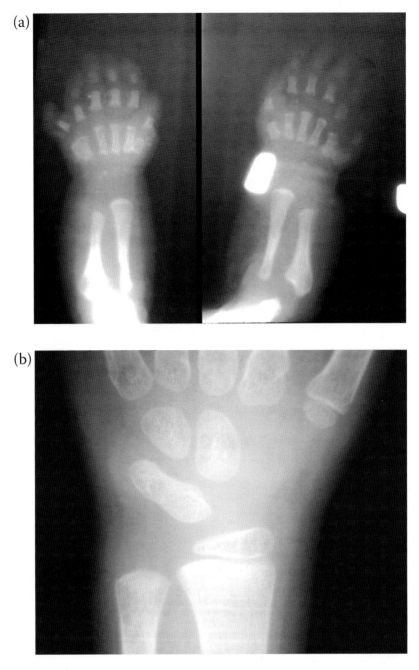

Figure 3.44 Some other skeletal findings in Ellis-van Creveld disease. (a) Progressive shortening of bones in the extremities. (b) Carpal fusion (carpe magnum).

(c)

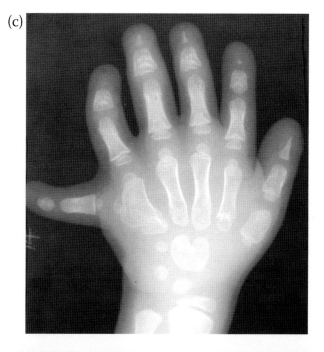

(d)

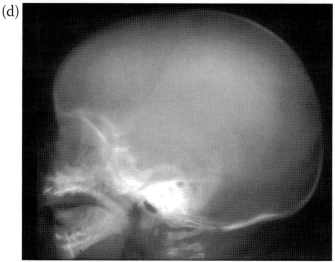

Figure 3.44 (*Continued*) Some other skeletal findings in Ellis-van Creveld disease. (c) Polydactyly. (d) Abnormal dentition (tooth buds) in infancy.

Congenital Indifference to Pain (Hereditary Sensory and Autonomic Neuropathy)

This fascinating but rare condition encompasses a spectrum of disorders characterized by dysfunctional perception of pain. All congenital, each form is caused by different genetic errors affecting specific phases of neurological development. The most common, type III, is an autosomal recessive familial disorder of children of Askenazi Jewish ancestry. Neonatal traits may include hypotonia, temperature instability, and a poor sucking reflex. There are variable responses to tactile, vibratory, and thermal stimuli. The condition may not be recognized early on. Injuries associated with teething may be the first indication.[72,73]

We have not seen examples of this disorder in the very young, although they do occur. Being insensitive to pain, they may present to emergency departments with repetitive injuries: burns, scrapes, lacerations, fractures, infections, etc. Repeated trauma may lead to the development of Charcot joints (Figure 3.45). Distal parts of extremities are extremely susceptible to repetitive trauma, which results in substantial mutilation and disability (Figure 3.46).

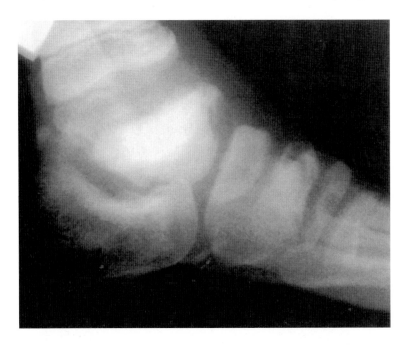

Figure 3.45 Seven-year-old female with congenital insensitivity to pain has a Charcot ankle due to repetitive unrecognized trauma. (Courtesy Deborah Iketa, MD.)

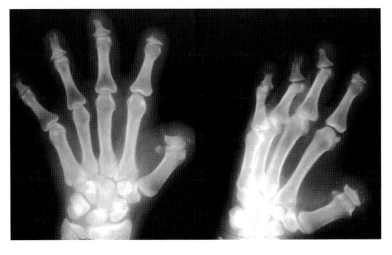

Figure 3.46 Hand of a 24-year-old woman with longstanding congenital insensitivity to pain, her fingers being slowly destroyed by repetitive trauma.

Obviously, differential diagnosis between accidental or nonaccidental trauma will be a problem only in the early years.

False Fractures

Factitious Splitting of the Femoral Head

The example (Figure 3.47) was a 5-year-old with a limp, the son of a professor in our medical school. The femoral head is divided longitudinally in this case into two segments by a strip of decreased density representing the synchondrosis between two ossification centers that developed in tandem, ventral to dorsal. Therefore it only is apparent in the "frog-leg" projection. It is a normal variant unrelated to any symptomatology or abnormality.[74] Why the child limped was never established, but he developed normally and without further difficulty related to either hip. (*Author's note*: According to my dictionary, "factitious" splitting is a misnomer, but who's going to argue with Silverman, Kuhn, and Caffey?)

(a)

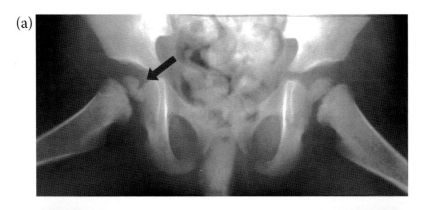

(b)

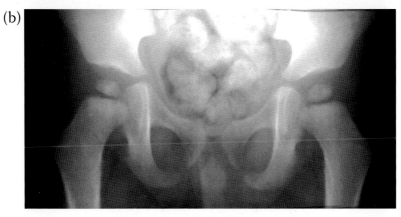

Figure 3.47 A 5-year-old male with a limp was examined with AP and frog-leg lateral views of both hips. (a) The frog-leg lateral shows a defect through the capital humeral epiphysis on the right (arrow), *the side away from the limp*. (b) The frontal view shows the hip to be normal.

Supernumerary Ossification Centers

The space between multiple ossification centers in a long bone, i.e., the clavicle, the pubis, can be confused with fracture[75] (Figure 3.48).

Panner's Disease

This affliction of the capitellum, the secondary ossification center on the radial or lateral side of the distal end of the humerus, was first described in 1929.[76] Since then, a range of opinions can be found as to the origin and exact nature of entity. It is said to result from a single traumatic event, or repetitive trauma, or aseptic necrosis, or lateral compression, or combinations of those. It has been called an osteochondrosis or an osteochondritis. It has been said to resemble such disparate lesions as Freiberg's infraction, Osgood-Schlatler's disease and Scheuermann's disease. It has been called osteochondritis dissecans, while other authors warn against that idea. It has been termed synonymous with Little Leaguer's elbow, which it is not.[77–80]

The radiological appearance begins with a slightly irregular, slightly dense margin of the capitellum, progressing to irregular or linear fissures in the periphery and centrum of the epiphysis (Figure 3.49). There usually is some collapse, but eventually there is reconstruction of the epiphysis to an essentially normal appearance.

Panner's disease is found in the dominant arm, almost exclusively in males between the ages of 5 and 12 (younger than the peak incidence of osteochondritis dissecans and Little Leaguer's elbow). It seems most likely that this entity is an osteochondrosis, perhaps with interference of blood supply, in association with reactive valgus stress and lateral compression from any sport or activity requiring a throwing motion.

The location of the lesion, and the age and activity of the victim are important. The deformation and fissuring/fracturing of the epiphysis is *not* indicative of nonaccidental trauma or abuse.

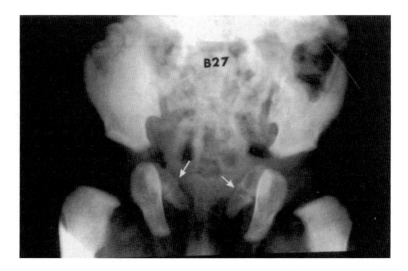

Figure 3.48 Lucency (arrows) between two ossification centers in the superior pubic ramus is a normal variant, not a fracture. Incidence of this finding is less than 1%.

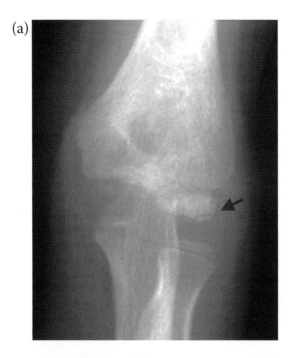

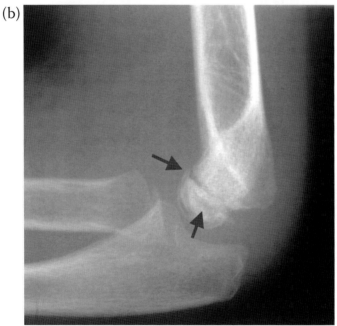

Figure 3.49 Panner's disease. (a) Frontal and (b) lateral views of the right elbow of an 8-year-old boy show some peripheral increase in density of the capitellar epiphysis, which is slightly flattened and deformed. Both central and marginal fissuring is seen (arrows).

Normal Fractures

There are certain injuries of the appendicular skeleton that are so common in the routine activities of normally developed children that they can be considered normal. That is, their discovery raises no red flag of suspicion of abuse unless occurring in a remarkably unusual context.

The "Toddler's Fracture"

The toddler's fracture refers to an occult oblique or spiral fracture of the tibia occurring in a child who is learning to walk[81] (Figure 3.50). Consequently, it commonly is seen in children 9 months to 3 years of age. New mechanical stresses on the tibia related to weight bearing and ambulation are responsible for these fractures. The newly walking child often has a pigeon-toed gait, and simply hanging a toe on any obstacle can produce torsional stress.

The child may present with sudden inability to walk or bear weight on one leg. These obliquely oriented undisplaced fractures in the lower half of the tibia diaphysis may be difficult to identify on the routine two-view radiography; additional views (obliques) may be necessary. Periosteal reactions on follow-up will confirm a missed or occult fracture.

Supracondylar Fracture of the Humerus

This most common fracture of the elbow in children is actually *transcondylar* through the coronoid fossa. It commonly is caused by a fall upon the outstretched hand, with displacement of the distal fragment posteriorly.[82] One-fourth are incomplete and may not be easily

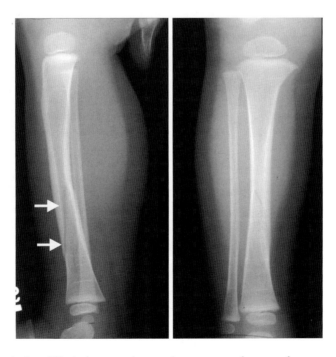

Figure 3.50 Typical toddler's fracture (arrows) seen on only one of two routine views. It is obique or spiral, hairline, undisplaced, nonangulated, with no overriding. Consequently, the fibula is not involved.

seen, but the displacement of the distal fragment and loss of anterior angulation of the distal articular surface is present almost always (Figure 3.51). This latter indication is demonstrated easily by extension of the anterior humeral line to show that it passes through or anterior to the anterior third of the capitellum in the lateral projection (Figure 3.52). They are *not* suggestive of nonaccidental trauma.

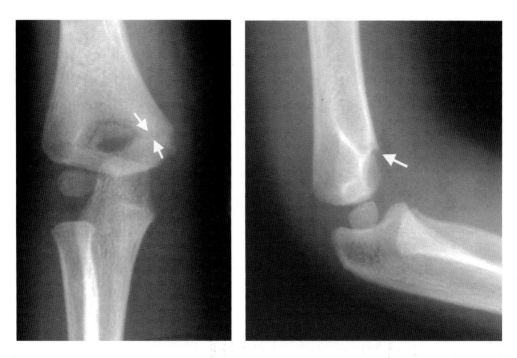

Figure 3.51 AP and lateral views of a child's elbow with a partially healed so-called supracondylar (transcondylar) fracture (arrows) of the distal metaphysis of the humerus.

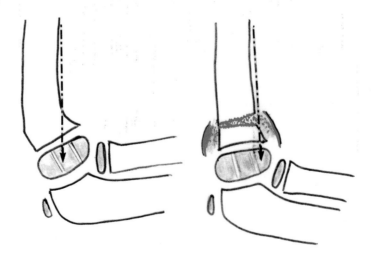

Figure 3.52 Schematic drawing showing (left) the anterior humeral line and (right) the usefulness of the anterior humeral line and the displacement of the anterior and posterior fat pads in detecting the fracture.

Little Leaguer's Elbow

Little Leaguer's elbow was described in 1960[83] as a separation of the apophysis of the medial epicondyle of the humerus in adolescent boys as a result of throwing a ball. It is caused by the explosive tug of the tendons of the flexor/pronator group on its insertion. It was found initially in Little League and Pony League pitchers, and is most common in the 9- to 14-year-old age group. Pitchers are most often victims because of their repetitive and concentrated throwing motion, but it is found in outfielders and can occur in other adolescents' sports activities replicating the critical stress on the flexor/pronator tendon, e.g., javelin or tennis. While the term is expressly limited to the specific ball-throwing activity,[83,84] avulsion of the medial epicondylar apophysis also is frequently encountered in this age group as a result of falling on the outstretched arm.

Although easily seen in the frontal projection of the elbow (Figure 3.53), the fragment located on the lateral projection may be displaced into the joint, requiring operative intervention (Figure 3.54).

Dislocations—Nontraumatic, Noninfectious, Nonabusive

As previously discussed, abusive dislocations are rare. They can result from jerking or shaking, but fractures are far more likely in the extremities. More dislocations in this age group are caused by direct accidental trauma or by the pressure of intracapsular blood, fluid, or exudate from inflammation or infection.

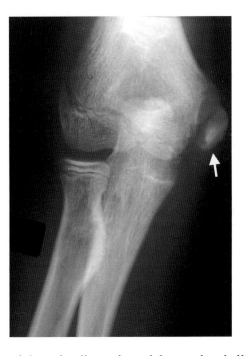

Figure 3.53 Frontal view of the right elbow of an adolescent baseball pitcher showing separation (arrow) of the secondary ossification center for the medial epicondylar apophysis (Little Leaguer's elbow).

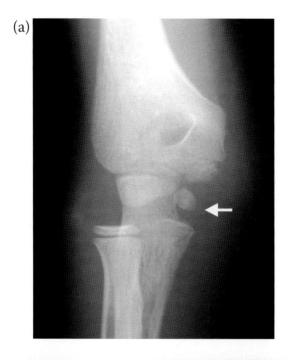

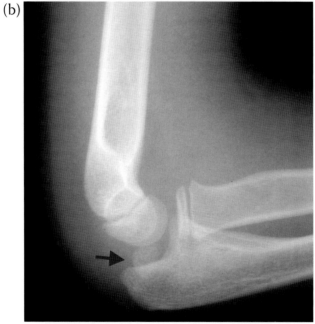

Figure 3.54 (a) Frontal and (b) lateral views of a Little Leaguer's elbow in which the ossification center for the medial epicondylar apophysis (arrows) is displaced into the elbow joint.

There are two entities exhibiting dislocations at multiple joints. These are unlikely to be confused with either accidental or nonaccidental trauma unless, on the unlikely occasion, a single joint or extremity is examined radiologically in the absence of history or context.

Arthrogryposis

Arthrogryposis multiplex congenita, first described by Otto in 1841, probably represents a spectrum of diseases rather than a single entity. Decreased fetal movement, of whatever cause, seems to be the common etiologic agent. These children have multiple joint contractures producing mostly valgus deformities and dislocations[85–87] (Figures 3.55 and 3.56).

There are associated bony deformities with hypoplasia and malformations of articular bones. Sensation and mentation are normal. There are soft tissue changes of diminished skin creases, webbing, and contracted and fibrotic periarticular tissues. Joint subluxations and dislocations are usually bilateral, symmetrical, and at multiple sites.

If more than one joint is examined, confusion with the traumatic etiology is extremely unlikely.

Larsen's Syndrome

A generalized mesenchymal disorder, Larsen's syndrome displays a multitude of congenital anomalies presenting at birth. The syndrome was first described in 1950 by Larsen and Schottstaedterbost.[88] They first described children with multiple congenital joint dislocations and characteristic facies with prominent foreheads, depressed nasal bridges, round facies, and wide-spaced eyes. The most characteristic finding is anterior dislocation of the tibia on the femur,[89] although dislocations may occur at any joint (Figure 3.57). Dislocation of the cervical

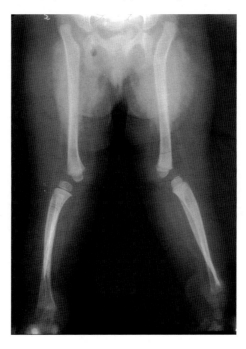

Figure 3.55 Lower extremities of a child with arthrogryposis showing bilateral dislocations at the hips, knees, and ankles.

Generally, children first exhibit symptoms in the first 5 to 6 months of life. Resolution is usually complete by 2 years of age. Infants present with hyperirritability, tender soft tissue swelling, and bulky periostitis of multiple bones. Multiple stages are seen as the process evolves. The keystone of the earliest phase is hyperostosis, which occurs in the outer cortex with expansion and is followed by resorption at the external or endochondral surface. Inflammatory changes typically extend into the adjacent soft tissues. In the subacute phase, the periosteum thickens and ossifies. The adjacent soft tissue inflammatory reaction also recedes. Removal of peripheral bone, initially from the inner surface, occurs during the late phase. Cortical remodeling also transpires at this time. The mandible, ribs, clavicle, and long bones are most affected, more or less in that order, but involvement has been reported in almost every bone, including the skull. Long-bone involvement usually is asymmetrical; mandibular, rib, and clavicular changes are more likely symmetrical (Figure 3.60).

Prostaglandin Therapy

Prostaglandin treatment is the standard of care for neonates with ductal dependent heart disease.[103,104] Often treatment is administered over a short period of time until definitive surgical treatment can be achieved; however, extended dispensation is required when surgical intervention is not immediately available or is unsuccessful. Common side effects include skin flushing, diarrhea, apnea, hypothermia, and subperiosteal bone formation.

The periosteal reaction or cortical hyperostosis is associated with prolonged prostaglandin therapy.[105] Development of periostitis has been reported with short-term therapy in as little as 2 weeks.[106] The bones most commonly affected are the long bones in the limbs: the femur, tibia, fibula, humerus, radius, ulna, ribs, and to a lesser extent, clavicles, scapula, and mandible[104–107](Figure 3.61). Cortical hyperostosis is always symmetric, but may not be

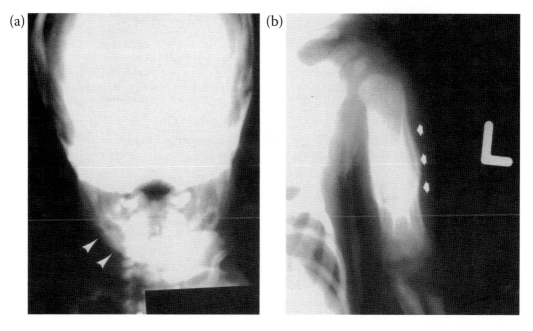

Figure 3.60 Caffey's disease (infantile cortical hyperostosis). Abundant hyperostotic periosteal reaction involving (a) the mandible, (b) the left humerus.

(c)

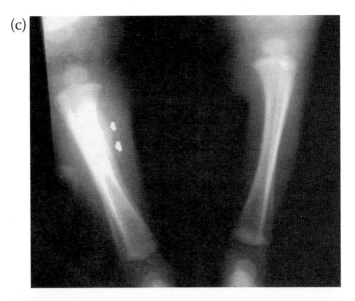

(d)

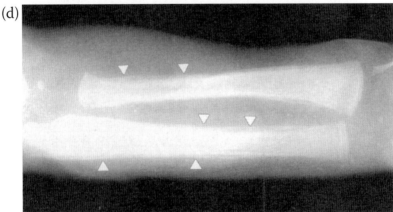

Figure 3.60 (*Continued*) Caffey's disease (infantile cortical hyperostosis). Abundant hyperostotic periosteal reaction involving (c) the right tibia, and (d) both bones of the left forearm.

uniform. Periostitis typically progresses with the duration of treatment but resolves after cessation of the medication.[103] The bones of these infants are poorly mineralized and may fracture with normal handling during routine nursery care.

Vitamin A Intoxication

The deleterious effects of excessive amounts of food containing vitamin A have been recognized for centuries. Gerrit de Veer wrote about his men becoming severely ill after eating polar bear liver while trying to reach Indonesia by the northern passage in 1597.[108] Today vitamin A in excessive amounts (>25,000 IU per day) is known to have detrimental effects, including decreased bone mineral density. Over an extended period of time, vitamin A toxicity can cause anorexia, bone pain, nausea, and weight loss.

Altering the balance of vitamin A metabolism can lead to increased bone resorption secondary to osteoclast stimulation, as well as periosteal bone formation.[109] Several studies

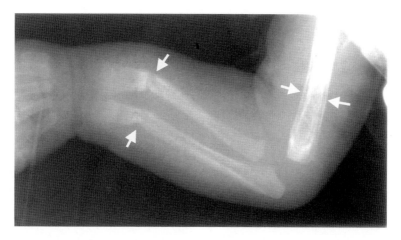

Figure 3.61 Upper extremity of an infant on prolonged prostaglandin therapy shows poor mineralization of all bones, periosteal reaction (arrows), and handling fractures of the distal radius and ulna (arrows).

have shown that increased dietary intake of vitamin A leads to decreased bone mineral density, increasing the relative risk of fracture.[110,111]

Although nonspecific, periosteal formation is typical in the metacarpals and metatarsals as well as the fibula, tibia, and ulna. In multiple bones, these changes may resemble multiple healing fractures. Additionally, these patients are at increased risk of pathologic fracture secondary to bone fragility.

In infants and children, vitamin overdose may be accidental, or attributable to hyper-anxious parenting (Figure 3.62).

Familial Hypophosphatemia

Familial hypophosphatemia is a rare metabolic bone disorder with characteristic radiologic findings that have been referred to as juvenile Paget's disease. The disease was first reported in 1973 by Caffey, who noted that "the basic casual mechanisms are enzymatic imbalances which causes an accelerated turnover of immature bone and collagen."[112] It is an autosomal recessive disorder with chronically elevated levels of alkaline phosphatase.[113] The elevated levels of alkaline phosphatase are secondary to destruction of bone by osteoclasts. Consequently, the process interferes with normal maturation of compact lamellar bone.

Patients present with motor abnormalities and fractures. Radiographically, there is enlargement of the head due to calvarial thickening, generalized cortical thickening, fusiform enlargement, and abnormal mineralization of the tubular bones with relative sparing of the epiphyses and endochondral bone (Figure 3.63). Abnormalities of long bones are apparent before calvarial thickening is appreciated.

Normal Physiological Periostitis of the Newborn

Physiological periostitis of the newborn is now a well-known radiological finding in normal infants aged 1–6 months.[114–116] It usually presents as a single thin layer of subperiosteal new bone involving the diaphyses of long bones (Figure 3.64); it may extend to the metaphyseal region but not all the way to the end of the bone. It is asystematic. Physiological

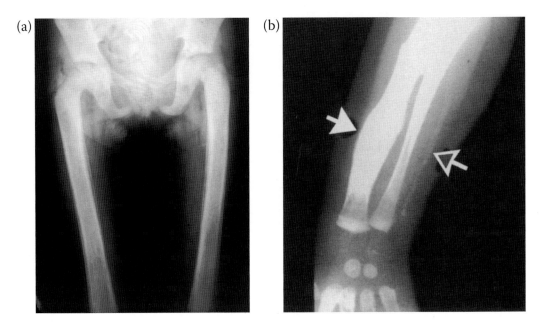

Figure 3.62 Hypervitaminosis A. (a) Subperiosteal new bone surrounding the femoral shafts of a 4-year-old child with vitamin A intoxication. Increased density near the ischial tuberosites suggests heterotopic calcification, perhaps related to hypercalcemia and vitamin D overdose as well. (b) Infant with vitamin A intoxication causing massive periosteal reaction about the midshaft of the radius (arrow); excessive vitamin D intake produced calcification of the ulnar artery (hollow arrow).

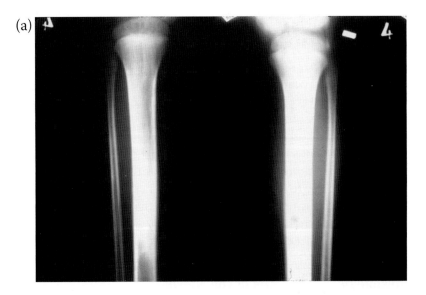

Figure 3.63 Hypophosphatemia. (a) Slightly fusiform periosteal thickening of the midshaft of both tibiae.

(b)

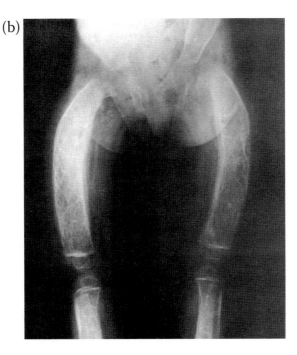

Figure 3.63 (Continued) Hypophosphatemia. (b) Massively thickened and bowed shafts of the femora, sparing the epiphyses. This appearance gives rise to the appellation juvenile Paget's disease, which, of course, it is not. Similar changes without bowing are present in the tibial shafts.

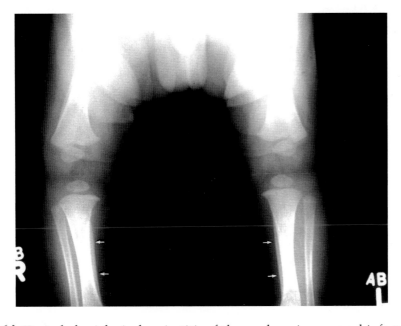

Figure 3.64 Typical physiological periostitis of the newborn in a normal infant. Note the symmetrical single fine line or layer of subperiosteal new bone alongside an otherwise normal bone.

periostitis invariably is symmetrical, although it may be more extensive on one limb than on its counterpart. The underlying bone will appear entirely normal. Therefore, if this finding is encountered unexpectedly upon examination of an extremity for some other reason, the opposite limb should be examined for a symmetrical finding to exclude trauma, given no other history or finding to suggest abuse.

The Spine

As previously discussed, nonaccidental trauma to the spine is rare without other associated injuries to the appendicular skeleton. However, a peculiar and complex sequence of chondrification and ossification of the spinal segments, when gone awry, can produce a host of malformations simulating trauma or its sequela. Consequently, an understanding of that process is essential for accurate evaluation of the sometimes confusing radiographic findings in the spines of infants and children.[117,118]

The formation of the primitive vertebral bodies commences on approximately the 24th day of fetal life around the notochord lying on the ventral aspect of the neural tube. The vertebral body forms first with two chondrification centers on either side of the notochord. Subsequently, anterior and posterior ossification centers develop in the centrum or body of the developing vertebra. Paired chondrification centers also appear in what will become the posterior neural arch of the vertebra (Figure 3.65).

Ideally, this process results in a single ossification center for the vertebral body and two lateral centers that eventually will fuse to form the neural arch, transverse processes, and spinous process. Failure of development or delayed fusion of any of these multiple anlagen can produce a host of vertebral malformations.

Additionally, anterior and posterior vascular channels supplying the vertebral bodies cause small radiolucent defects (Figure 3.66). The anterior channels gradually disappear. The posterior channels may be apparent even in adults.[119]

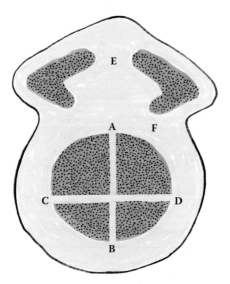

Figure 3.65 Schematic representation of the chondrification centers that ultimately form the vertebral body and the paired lateral centers that will form the posterior neural arch, including the transverse and spinous processes.

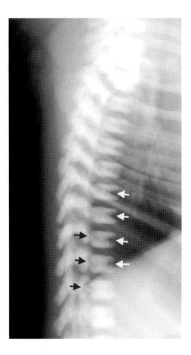

Figure 3.66 Infantile vertebrae showing anterior (white arrows) and posterior (black arrows) lucent defects where vascular channels enter and leave the vertebral bodies. Although the anterior channels are more obvious, they will disappear; the posterior "grooves" may persist into the adult (which may explain why most vertebral metastases start in the posterior part of the vertebral body[119]).

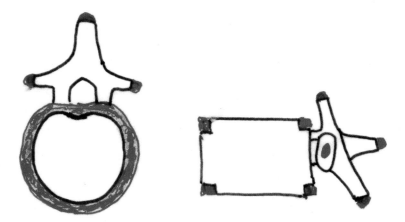

Figure 3.67 Schematic top and lateral view of a developing vertebra showing sites of secondary apophyseal centers. Of course they are not visible until calcification begins. Therefore, the ring epiphyses at the vertebral end plates will appear as squared notches at the vertebral corners until calcified.

In late subteenage years, annular crescentic epiphyses appear at superior and inferior margins of the end plates of the vertebral bodies. At about the time of puberty, secondary ossification centers develop at the tips of the spinous process, the transverse processes, and the articular processes. These are not to be confused with "chip" fractures (Figure 3.67).

Coronal Cleft Vertebra

Coronal cleft vertebra is a common finding in a pediatric radiology practice, but may be confusing when encountered by physicians in other disciplines.[120,121] It is seen incidentally in normal healthy children who are imaged with the body in a lateral position. It represents a delayed fusion of anterior and posterior ossification centers (along the line C-D in Figure 3.65) in the vertebral body. Failure of notochord regression has been implicated by some authors.[122] It is of no clinical consequence and will disappear with normal growth and maturation of the child. Coronal clefts, when seen, usually are present at multiple levels (Figure 3.68).

A *spurious coronal cleft* appearance is sometimes seen if the attempted lateral view is somewhat obliqued. The neural arch does not fuse with that vertebral body until the third to fourth year of life. Space between ossified portions of the arch and the ossified vertebral body (at Figure 3.65F) can resemble a coronal cleft at first glance (Figure 3.69). Unfortunately, it can also be confused with a fracture. Note that the margins of the defect are corticated, and a fracture margin will not be.

Vertical or Sagittal Cleft

If fusion fails or is delayed along the line A-B in Figure 3.65, a vertical cleft can occur but is rare and often is not a vertical cleft at all, but a spina bifida. A true vertical cleft should remain centered in the vertebral body on frontal views and may disappear on slight or moderate rotation of the body (Figure 3.70). If persistent until weight bearing begins in the

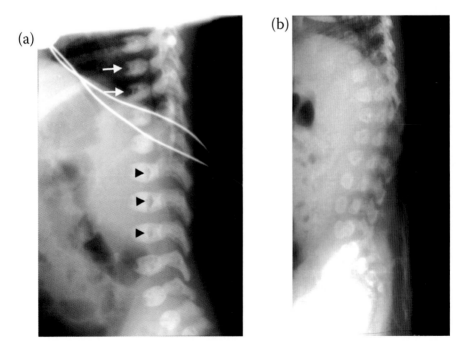

Figure 3.68 Coronal cleft vertebra. (a) Infant with coronal clefts (arrowheads) and persistent anterior vascular grooves (arrows) that are disappearing from the caudad upward. (b) Slightly older infant with coronal clefts. The vascular grooves have disappeared. (Coronal clefts represent failure of fusion on the line C-D in Figure 3.65.)

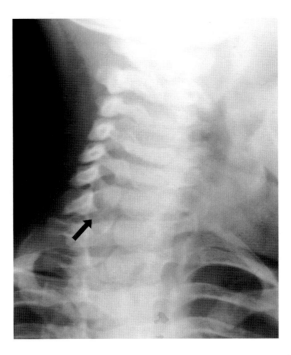

Figure 3.69 Normal space (arrow) between the neural arch and the vertebral body until fusion occurs in the third or fourth year of life, seen mostly on oblique views, whether malpositioned lateral views or intentional. (This is located at F in Figure 3.65.)

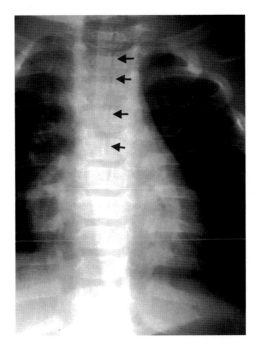

Figure 3.70 Vertical or sagittal clefts (arrows). (This represents failure of fusion along line A-B in Figure 3.65.)

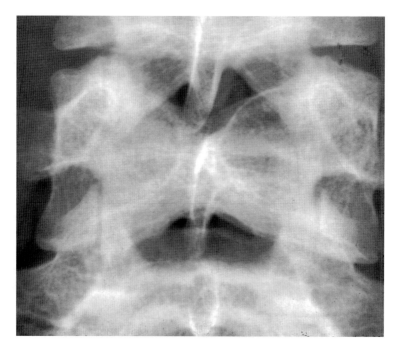

Figure 3.71 Butterfly vertebra.

upright position, the two lateral halves may spread and produce the "butterfly" vertebra seen occasionally in adults[118] (Figure 3.71). Again, this failure of fusion is considered by some to result from persistent notochord remnants.[117] The two wedges making up the butterfly may be asymmetrical with resultant scoliosis.

Hemivertebrae

If one of the lateral chondrification centers fails in normal development, a hemivertebra results. These can cause scoliosis if unbalanced by an adjacent contralateral hemivertebra or overgrowth of the contralateral half of a normal vertebra above or below the hemivertebra (Figure 3.72). Rib anomalies may accompany thoracic hemivertebrae.

Much rarer is failure of development of the anterior ossification center producing a dorsal hemivertebra. This causes a sharp angular kyphosis (gibbus deformity) with potential for serious impingement on the spinal cord or spinal nerves.

Spina Bifida

The two primary ossification centers that develop into the posterior neural arch gradually fuse to form the spinous process during the second year. This normal defect between the unfused center is seen on frontal radiographs and can be confused with the rare vertical cleft, as it will be projected behind the vertebral body. However, slight rotator variations in positing of the trunk will shift the radiographic defect off the central axes of the vertebral body, thus revealing its posterior location (Figure 3.73). Spina bifida presents, most often in the lower lumbar spine, in about one-third of adults.[123]

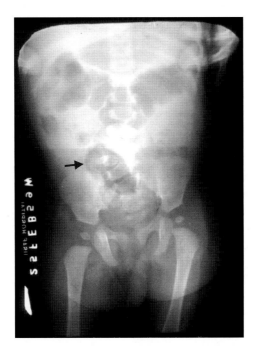

Figure 3.72 A hemivertebra balanced by overgrowth or hypertrophy of the contralateral halves of the vertebrae above and below. (The body always tries to keep the eyes level, hence the balanced hemivertebra or the *s*-shaped scoliosis.)

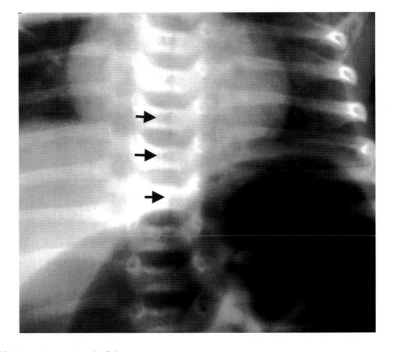

Figure 3.73 Lumbar spina bifida.

Physiological Sclerosis of the Newborn

Clefts and defects in the infant spine may be more obvious or accentuated by physiological sclerosis in some newborns. The skeleton appears more dense because the bones contain more compact bone and less spongiosa and medullary canal. The thicker cortex is more dense. This is a transient phenomenon and disappears in a few days[124] (Figure 3.74).

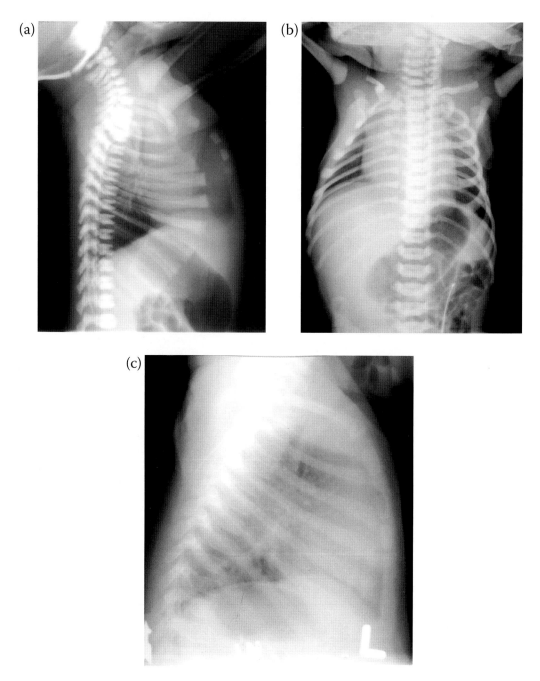

Figure 3.74 (a, b) Physiologic sclerosis in a newborn. (c) Same child, 4 weeks later.

Hurler Syndrome

The classic inferior beaking of a lumbar vertebra in Hurler syndrome closely resembles the profile of the compression fracture with anterosuperior notching previously described with intentional trauma (Figure 3.75). However, unless the spine is seen in isolation, there will be no confusion because of the myriad skeletal abnormalities found in this syndrome, literally from head to toe, including J-shaped sella (Figure 3.76); flattened mandibular condyle,

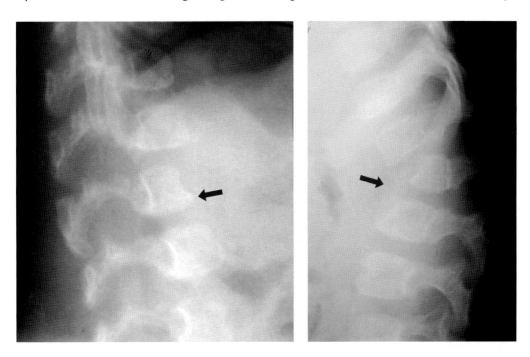

Figure 3.75 Two examples of the typical anteroinferior beaking of the vertebral body in Hurler syndrome. One or more lumbar vertebrae may be involved, usually L1-L3, often with associated gibbus deformity, as best illustrated here in example b.

Figure 3.76 Lateral skull with typical J-shaped sella turcica of Hurler syndrome.

spinal gibbus at the level of the vertebral body deformity (Figure 3.75b); oar-shaped ribs (Figure 3.77); varus deformity of humeral and femoral necks, tilting of the distal ends of the radius and ulna toward each other (Figure 3.78); pointing of the proximal ends of the metacarpals, and bullet-shaped phalanges pointing distally (Figure 3.79); and similar but less marked deformation in the feet.[125,126]

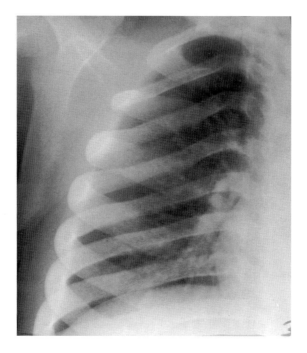

Figure 3.77 Flattened, widened anterior rib ends in Hurler syndrome are likened to paddles or oars.

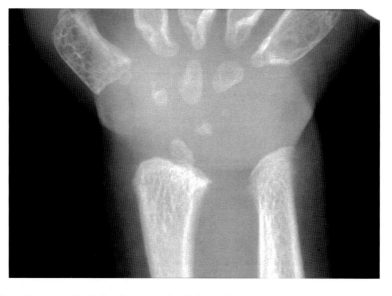

Figure 3.78 In-facing tilt of the distal ends of the radius and ulna in Hurler syndrome.

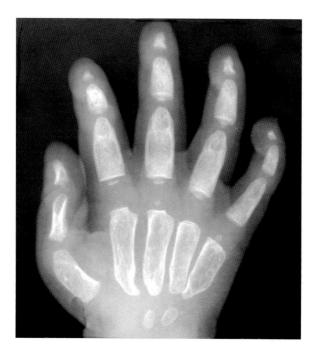

Figure 3.79 Hurler syndrome typical hand. Note the proximally pointed ends of the metacarpals, and the distally pointed bullet-shaped phalanges.

Stippled Epiphyses

In the spine, the anterior portion of the vertebral bodies is affected and ossification may be delayed, producing a temporary deformity.[39] The vascular channels may be accentuated. In the sacrum, the irregular calcification may stimulate traumatic deformities such as those inflicted by slamming the baby down on his or her bottom (Figure 3.80).

Infarction

Infarction of blood supply to the growing vertebral body can produce deformity. This can be related to disease, i.e., sickle cell disease, or infection, i.e., tuberculosis or meningococcemia. Rarely seen in the infant, these deformities may be encountered in older children. The most common deformity is a biconcave cupping of the vertebral end plates, which resembles a compression fracture such as seen in weakened or osteoporotic bone. The infarcts, especially in sickle cell disease, present as a more central end-plate depression with squared-off sides, sometimes called the "Lincoln log" deformity (Figure 3.81).

Vertebra Plana

We have seen that compression fractures can flatten the vertebral body to some degree (Figure 2.42). When the vertical height of the body is substantially reduced by nontraumatic conditions it is called vertebra plana (Figures 3.82 and 3.83).

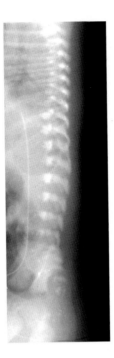

Figure 3.80 Lateral view of the spine of a newborn with stippled epiphyses.

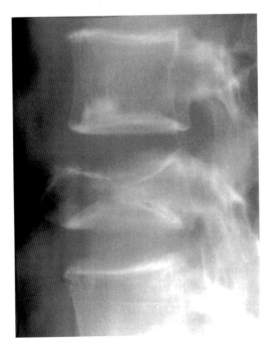

Figure 3.81 Meningococcemia. The vascular injury to the vertebral end plates by the coagulopathy of this disease creates the deformation resembling the biconclave compression-type fracture.

(a)   (b)

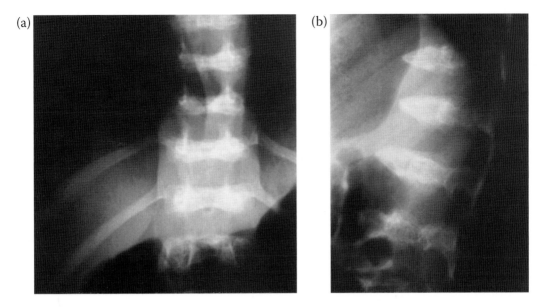

Figure 3.82 Probable Kozloski's spondylometaphyseal chondrodysplasia.[127] (a) The vertebrae appear as flattened (vertebra plana) in the frontal projection. (b) In the lateral view they are flattened and pointed, somewhat like the vertebral deformity in Morquio's syndrome.[128]

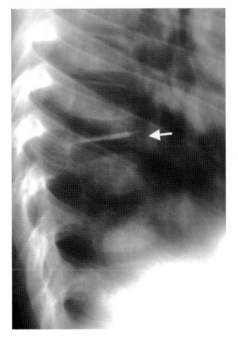

Figure 3.83 The classic example of vertebra plana is found most often in children with the Hand-Schüller-Christian type of Langerhans cell histiocytosis.[129]

The Skull

Increased Pressure?

Construction of the newborn skull is one of nature's most daunting and complex tasks. Some of the parts come from enchondral bone formation and some from intramembranous ossification. Some components are paired with mirror images and some are unpaired. There are at one time or another seven fontanelles present rather than the two (anterior and posterior) with which we are reasonably familiar. The spaces—future joints—between adjacent components originally are widely spaced and join slowly, almost reluctantly, in joints we call sutures, and the process is not finalized until the mid-twenties. The sutures at first are widely spaced, and gradually grow closer before apposition and fusion—unless re-expanded by intracranial pressure. There are no dependable measurements to determine whether the sutural width is normal at any given time. Hence evaluation depends on the "mind's-eye view" and memory bank of an experienced observer. When in doubt, ask for help, and rely on other evidence of increased intracranial pressure, especially those possibly the sequellae of trauma, whether accidental or intentional.

Fractures

Fissures or accessory sutures may be confused with fracture in the infant.[130] The following three are most likely to be confused:

1. The *metopic suture* is easiest to deal with. It is squarely in the midline of the frontal bone and may be present for years.
2. The *intraparietal suture* or *parietal fissure* is more difficult. The parietal bone is formed from two centers, and sometimes the junction and fusion are incomplete, usually posteriorly about midway up the lambdoid suture. It occasionally will extend longitudinally across the parietal bone as a linear area of diminished density; usually it is a short lucent "defect" extending a short distance upward and anteriorly from the lambdoid suture (Figure 3.84).
3. The *mendosal* or *interoccipital suture* is a paired complete or partial cleft between the superior and basilar halves of the occipital bone found on both the lateral view and the Townes or basilar view (Figure 3.85).

Wormian Bones

Intersutural or wormian bones are found in many skulls, either incidentally or in association with a wide variety of conditions. Consequently, they have no significant specificity. They occur most commonly in the lambdoid sutures. They are not to be confused with comminuted fractures (Figure 3.86).

Cephalohematoma

Cephalohematoma is a common lesion of newborn infants that may develop from traction applied to the scalp of the fetus as it is dragged through the pelvic birth canal. The scalp

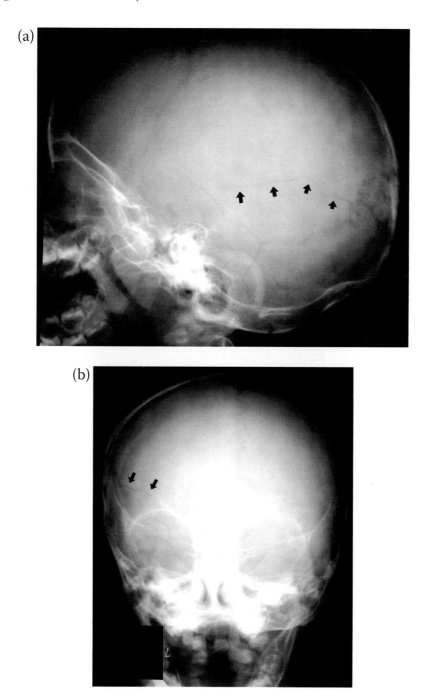

Figure 3.84 (a) Lateral view and (b) frontal view of skull showing interparietal suture or fissure (arrows).

is separated from the pericranium and bleeding ensues but is limited to the periosteal attachments at the suture lines *and does not* cross them. The lesion is commonly located over the parietal bone, although frontal and occipital bones occasionally are involved. Large male babies are more likely to have cephalohematoma. Forceps delivery triples the incidence.

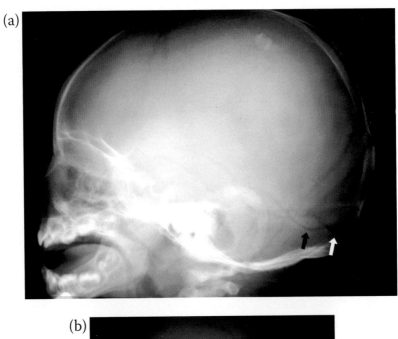

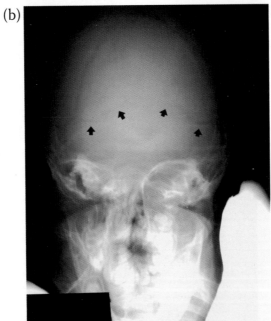

Figure 3.85 (a) Lateral view and (b) frontal view of skull showing mendosal suture (arrows).

Underlying skull fractures occur with cephalohematoma in fewer than 25% of cases. (The incidence seems to be diminishing as obstetrical practices change. When present, the fractures are linear and almost exclusively in the parietal bones.)[131]

Presenting on radiographs initially as a soft tissue mass, the cephalohematoma calcifies, first peripherally, with a classic radiological appearance (Figure 3.87). The lesion gradually will resorb and remodel to a virtual vanishing point.

Cephalohematoma occurring over the occipital bone can be confused clinically with a meningocele.

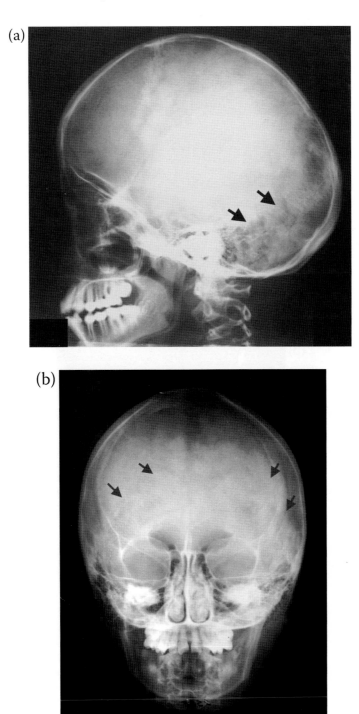

Figure 3.86 Multiple wormian bones in the lambdoid sutures in (a) lateral and (b) frontal views of the skull.

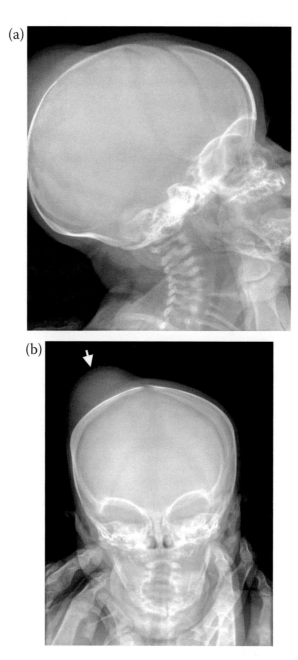

Figure 3.87 (a, b) Classic appearance of a right parietal cephalohematoma. Later a peripheral shell of calcification will appear. Resorption and remodeling eventually will restore the calvaria to essentially normal configuration and appearance.

Leptomeningeal Cyst

Sometimes the trauma causing a linear skull fracture, from whatever cause, also tears the dura matter. This allows meninges, or even brain, to herniate into the fracture, thus inhibiting fracture healing. The pulsation of cerebrospinal fluid can enlarge the fracture. Large calvarial defects with substantial fluid and soft tissue herniation can ensue and may require surgical intervention[132] (Figure 3.88).

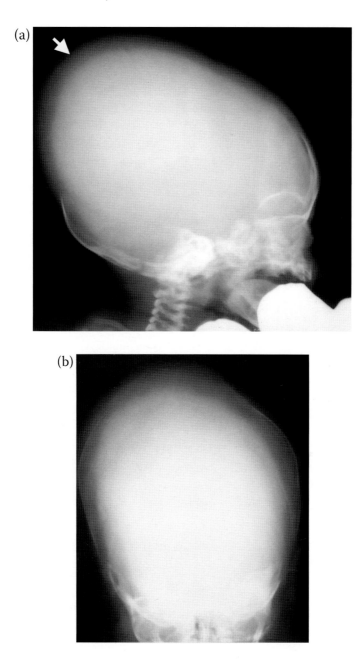

Figure 3.88 (a, b) Infant skull with a huge protruding soft tissue mass representing a lepto-meningeal cyst.

Abnormal Fetal Packing

Prenatal molding of the fetal skull may be produced by prolonged pressure of a fetal limb against the head, often in association with oligohydramnios. Fetal feet or hands are the common offenders and can even be easily positioned into the cranial depression after delivery. The sides of the head are most often involved (unilaterally or bilaterally), but the forehead can also be affected. Lack of any swelling, discoloration, tenderness, etc., excludes depressed fractures[133,134] (Figure 3.89).

(a)

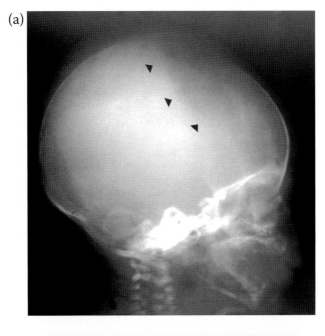

(b)

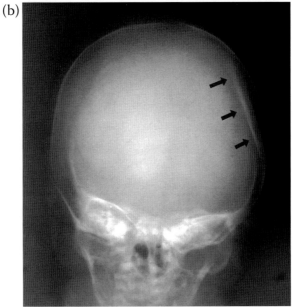

Figure 3.89 (a, b) Unilateral left frontoparietal depression in the skull as a result of abnormal fetal packing in utero (arrowheads).

Ping-Pong Ball Fractures

Pressure against the fetal skull during parturition by pelvic bone, forceps, and even the obstetrician's hand, can indent the skull in a smooth hemispheric or saucer-like depression without any associated fractures (Figure 3.90). This has been likened to the depression one can make in a ping-pong ball without rupturing it. The cranial curvature can usually be restored by gentle pressure at the periphery of the lesion or by suction, e.g., with a breast pump.[135]

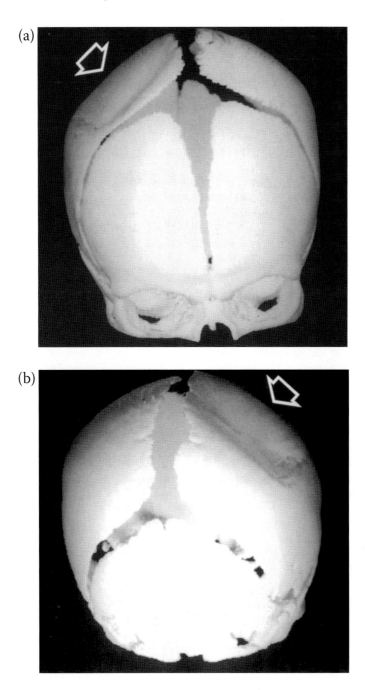

Figure 3.90 (a, b) Anterior and posterior views of a 3D CT reconstruction of a newborn skull demonstrated a "ping-pong ball" fracture. In this particular case, the fetal skull was already entering the birth canal when a cesarean section was begun. The obstetrician successfully pushed it back into the uterus from below, but produced this ping-pong ball fracture in so doing.

References

1. Olmedo, J.M., Yiannias, J.A., Windgassen, E.B., and Gornet, M.K. 2006. Scurvy: A disease almost forgotten. *Int J Dermatol* 45:909–13.
2. Fain, O. 2005. Musculoskeletal manifestations of scurvy. *Joint Bone Spine* 72:124–28.
3. Meschan, I. 1962. *Synopsis of roentgen signs*. WB Saunders, Philadelphia, 96.
4. Moncrieff, M., and Eadahunsi, T.O. 1974. Congenital rickets due to maternal vitamin D deficiency. *Arch Dis Child* 49:810–11.
5. Stewart, G.M., and Rosenberg, N.M. 1996. Conditions mistaken for child abuse: Part 1. *Pediatr Emerg Care* 12:116–21.
6. Silverman, F.N., and Kuhn, J., eds. 1993. *Caffey's pediatric x-ray diagnosis: An integrated imaging approach*, 9th ed. Mosby, St. Louis, 1746–54.
7. Hahn, T.J., Hendin, B.A., and Sharp, C.R. 1972. Effect of chronic anticonvulsant therapy on serum 25-hydroxycalciferol levels in adults. *N Engl J Med* 287:900–4.
8. Bouillon, R., Reynaert, J., and Claes, J.H. 1975. The effect of anticonvulsant therapy on serum levels of 25-hydroxy-vitamin D, calcium and parathyroid hormone. *J Clin Endocrinol Metab* 41:1130–35.
9. Menkes, J.H., Alter, M., Steigleder, G.K., et al. 1962. A sex-linked recessive disorder with retardation of growth, peculiar hair, and focal cerebral and cerebellar degeneration. *Pediatrics* 29:764–69.
10. Kodama, H., Murata, Y., and Kobayashi, M. 1999. Clinical manifestations and treatment of Menkes disease and its variants. *Pediatr Int* 41(4):423–29.
11. Wesenberg, R.L., Gwinn, J.L., and Barnes, G.R., Jr. 1969. Radiological findings in the kinky-hair syndrome. *Radiology* 92:500–6.
12. Arita, J.H., Faria, E.C., Peruchi, M.M., et al. 2009. Menkes disease as a differential diagnosis of child abuse. *Arq Neuropsiquiatr* 67(2B):507–9.
13. Lazoff, S.G., Ryback, J.J., Parker, B.R., et al. 1975. Skeletal dysplasia, occipital horns, diarrhea and obstructive uropathy: A new hereditary syndrome. *Birth Defects* 11:71–74.
14. Seay, A.R., Bray, P.F., Wing, D.S., Thompson, J.A., Bale, J.F., and Williams, D.M. 1979. CT scans in Menkes disease. *Neurology* 29:304–12.
15. Chelly, J., Tumer, Z., Tonnesen, T., et al. 1993. Isolation of a candidate gene for Menkes disease and metal binding protein. *Nat Genet* 3:14–19.
16. Stewart, C.M., Norman, M., and Rosenburg, M. 1996. Conditions mistaken for child abuse: Part I. *Pediatr Emerg Care* 12:116–221.
17. McLean, S. 1931. The roentgenographic and pathologic aspects of congenital osseous syphilis. *Am J Dis Child* 41:130–52.
18. McLean, S. 1931. The correlation of the roentgenographic and pathologic aspects of congenital osseous syphilis. *Am J Dis Child* 41:363–95.
19. McLean, S. 1931. The correlation of the clinical picture with the osseous lesions of congenital syphilis as shown by x-rays. *Am J Dis Child* 41:887–922.
20. Rasool, M.N., and Govender, S. 1989. The skeletal manifestations of congenital syphilis: A review of 197 cases. *J Bone Jt Surg* 71B(5):752–55.
21. Kim, S.J., Lee, S.W., and Rhim, J.W. 2009. A case of congenital syphilis mistaken for possible child abuse. *Korean J Pediatr* 52:710–12.
22. Williams, H.J., and Carey, L.S. 1996. Rubella embryopathy: Roentgenographic features. *AJR Am J Roentgenol* 97:92–99.
23. Graham, C.B., Thal, A., and Wassum, C.S. 1970. Rubella-like bone change in congenital cytomygalic inclusion disease. *Radiology* 94:39.
24. Kleinman, P.K. 1991. Schmid-like metaphyseal chrondrodysplasia simulating child abuse. *AJR Am J Roentgenol* 156:576–78.
25. Schmid, F. 1949. Beitrag zur dysostosis enchrondralis metaphysaria. *Monatsschr Kinderheilk* 97:393.

26. Alves, C., Sobral, M.M., and Ney-Oliveria, F. 2010. Metaphyseal chondrodysplasia, Schmid-type. *J Pediatr Endocrinol Metab* 23:331–32.

27. Lachman, R.S. 1996. *Skeletal dysplasias*. In Taybi, H., and Lachman, R.S., *Radiology of syndromes, metabolic disorders, and skeletal dysplasias*. Mosby-Yearbook, St. Louis, 851–58.

28. Tachdijian, M.O. 1972. *Pediatric orthopedics*. W.B. Saunders, Philadelphia, 425–27.

29. Wessels, V., Hesseling, P.B., and Van der Merwe, H.P. 1996. Bone involvement in childhood ALL. *East Afr Med J* 73:126–28.

30. Masera, G., Carnelli, V., Ferrari, M., et al. 1977. Prognostic significance of radiological bone involvement in childhood acute lymphoblastic leukaemia. *Arch Dis Child* 52:530–33.

31. Rogalsky, R.J., Black, G.B., and Reed, M.H. 1986. Orthopaedic manifestations of leukemia in children. *J Bone Jt Surg Am* 68:494–501.

32. Grogan, D.P., Love, S.M., Ogden, J.A., Millar, E.A., and Johnson, L.O. 1989. Chondro-osseous growth abnormalities after meningococcemia. *J Bone Jt Surg* 71A:920–28.

33. Dotter, W.E. 1953. Little Leaguer's shoulder: A fracture of the proximal epiphyseal cartilage on the humerus due to baseball pitching. *Guthrie Clin Bull* 23:68–72.

34. Tullos, H.S., and King, J.W. 1972. Lesions of the pitching arm in adolescents. *JAMA* 220:264.

35. Fraser, D. 1957. Hypophosphatasia. *Am J Med* 22:730–46.

36. Shohat, M., Rimoin, D.L., Gruber, H.E., and Lachman, R.S. 1991. Perinatal lethal hypophosphatasia; clinical radiologic and morphologic findings. *Pediatr Radiol* 21:421–27.

37. Pauli, R.M., Modaff, P., Sipes, S.L., and Whyte, M.P. 1999. Mild hypophosphatasia mimicking severe osteogenesis imperfect in utero: Bent but not broken. *Am J Genet* 86:434–48.

38. Mornet, E. 2007. Hypophosphatasia. *Ophanet Jo Rare* 2:40.

39. Brogdon, B.G., and Crow, N.E. 1958. Chondrodyslrophia calcificans congenital. *AJR Am J Roentgenol* 80:443–48.

40. Bilo, R.A.C., Robbin, S.G., and van Rijn, R.R. 2010. *Forensic aspects of paediatric fractures*. Springer, Berlin, 107–9.

41. Morris, S., Cassidy, N., Stephens, M., McCormack, D., and McManus, F. 2002. Birth associated femoral fractures: Incidence and outcome. *J Pediatr Orthop* 22:27–30.

42. Gordon, A.B., Fletcher, M.A., and MacDonald, G.M. 1999. *Neonatology, pathophysiology, and management of the newborn*, 5th ed. Lippincott Williams & Wilkins, Philadelphia, 1280–81.

43. Perlow, J.H., Wigton, T., Hart, J., Strassner, H.T., et al. 1996. Birth trauma: A five year review of incidence and associated perinatal factors. *J Reprod Med* 41:754–60.

44. Toker, A., Perry, H., Cohen, E., and Krymko, H. 2009. Cesarean section and the risk of fractured femur. *Isr Med Assoc J* 11:413–18.

45. Bilo, R.A.C., Robbin, S.G., and van Rijn, R.R. 2010. *Forensic aspects of paediatric fractures*. Springer, Berlin, 26–28.

46. Picket, W.J., Johnson, J.F., and Enzenauer, R.W. 1982. Case report 192. Neonatal fractures mimicking abuse secondary to physical therapy. *Skeletal Radiol* 8:85–86.

47. Hymel, K.P., and Jenny, C. 1996. Abusive spiral fracture of the humerus: A videotape exception. *Arch Pediatr Adolesc Med* 150:226–28.

48. Bowley, D.M.G., Loveland, J., and Pitcher, G.J.J. 2003. Tibial fracture as a complication of intraosseous infusion during pediatric resuscitation. *Trauma* 55:786–87.

49. Harty, M.P., and Kao, S.C. 2002. Intraosseous vascular access defect: Fracture mimic in the skeletal survey for child abuse. *Pediatr Radiol* 32:188–90.

50. Brogdon, B.G., and McDowell, J.D. 2011. Abuse of intimate partners and the elderly: An overview. In Thali, M.J., Viner, M.D., and Brogdon, B.G., eds., *Brogdon's forensic radiology*, 2nd ed. CRC Press, Boca Raton, FL, 288–91.

51. McPhee, S.J., Lingappa, V.R., Ganong, W.F., and Lang, J.D. 1995. *Pathophysiology of disease*. Prentice Hall, Upper Saddle River, NJ.

52. Byers, P.H. 1993. Osteogenesis imperfect. In Royce, P.M., and Steinmann, B., *Connective tissue and its heritable disorders: Molecular, genetic, and medical aspects*. Wiley-Liss, New York, 317–50.

53. Wright, J.T., and Thornton, J.B. 1983. Osteogenesis imperfect with dentinogenesis imperfect: A mistaken case of child abuse. *Pediatr Dent* 5:207–9.

54. Paterson, C.R., Burns, J., and McAllion, S.J. 1993. Osteogenesis imperfect: The distinction from child abuse and the recognition of a variant form. *Am J Med Genet* 45:187–92.

55. Miller, M.E. 1999. Temporary brittle bone disease: A true entity? *Semin Perinatol* 23:174–82.

56. Paterson, C.R., and Monk, E.A. 2000. Long-term follow up of children thought to have had temporary brittle bone disease. *Osteoporos Int* 11(Suppl. 4):S47–48.

57. Paterson, C.R. 2004. Corruption and miscarriage of justice in childcare case. Lecture at NCHR's Symposium, Gothenburg, Sweden. http://www.nkmr.org/english/bone_disease_that_lead_to_false_allegations_of_child_abuse... (accessed March 22, 2011).

58. Sprigg, A. Temporary brittle bone disease versus suspected non-accidental trauma. *Arch Dis Child*, doi.10.1136/adc.2009.180463.

59. Ablin, D.S., Greenspan, A., Reinhart, M., and Grix, A. 1990. Differentiation of child abuse from osteogenesis imperfect. *AJR Am J Roentgenol* 154:1035–46.

60. Chapman, S., and Hall, C.M. 1997. Non-accidental injury or brittle bone. *Pediatr Radiol* 27:106–10.

61. Marcovitch, H., and Mughal, M.Z. 2010. Cases do not support brittle bone disease. *Acta Paediatr* 99:485–86.

62. Dwyer, O. 2004. GMC strikes off proponent of temporary brittle bone disease. *BMJ* 328:604.

63. Vitale, M.G., and Gaha, D.I. 2002. Orthopaedic manifestations of neurofibromatoris in children: An update. *Clin Orthop* 10–18.

64. Boyd, H.B., and Sage, F.P. 1958. Congenital psuedoarthrosis of the tibia. *J Bone Joint Surg* 40A:1245.

65. Brunetti-Pierri, N., Doty, S.B., Hicks, J., et al. 2008. Generalized metabolic bone disease in neurofibromatosis type 1. *Mol Genet Metab* 94(1):105–11.

66. Holt, S.F. 1978. Neurofibromatosis in children: The Neuhauser lecture. *AJR* 130:615–39.

67. Cheema, F.I., Grissom, L.E., and Harcke, H.T. 2003. Radiographic characteristics of lower-extremity bowing in children. *Radiographics* 23:871–80.

68. Silverman, F.N., and Kuhn, J.P. 1990. *Essentials of Caffey's pediatric x-ray diagnosis.* Year Book, Chicago, 940.

69. Ellis, R.W., and van Creveld, S. 1940. A syndrome characterized by ectodermaldysplasia, poly-dactyly, chondrodyplasia and congenital morbus cardia. *Arch Dis Child* 15:65–84.

70. Wood, W.L., Lovell, R.B., Winter, R.T., et al. 2006. *Lovell and Winter's pediatric orthopaedics.* Lippincott Williams & Wilkins, Philadelphia.

71. Baujat, G., and Le Merrer, M. 2007. Ellis-van Creveld syndrome. *Orphanet J Rare Dis* 2:27–31.

72. Axelrod, F.B., and Gold-von Simson, G. 2007. Hereditary sensory and autonomic neuropa-thies: Types II, III and IV. *Orphanet J Rare Dis* 39:1172.

73. Wegli, D., Parvari, R., Katz, K., et al. 2002. Congenital insensitivity to pain: Orthopaedic mani-festations. *J Bone Jt Surg* 84A:252–57.

74. Silverman, F.N., and Kuhn, J.P., eds. 1993. *Caffey's pediatric x-ray diagnosis: An integrated imag-ing approach*, 4th ed. Mosby, St. Louis, 1498.

75. Caffey, J., and Madell, S.H. 1956. Ossification of the pubis bone at birth. *Radiology* 67:436–50.

76. Panner, H.J. 1929. A peculiar affection of the capetulum humeri, resembling Calve-Perths disease of the hip. *Acta Radiol* 10:234–42.

77. Rogers, L.F. 1992. *Radiology of skeletal trauma*, 2nd ed., vol. 2. Churchill Livingstone, New York, 765–66.

78. Adams, J.E. 1965. Injury to the throwing arm: a study of traumatic changes in the elbow joints of boy baseball players. *Calif Med* 102:127–32.

79. Lee, P., Hunter, T.B., and Taljanovic, M. 2004. Musculoskeletal colloquialisms: How did we come up with those names? *Radiographics* 29:1009–27.

80. Daniel, W.W. 1989. Panner's disease. *Arthritis Rheum* 32:1341–42.

81. Dunbar, J.S., Owen, H.F., Nogrady, M.B., et al. 1993. Obscure tibial fracture of infants: The toddler's fracture. *J Can Assoc Radiol* 15:136–44.

82. Kirks, D.R. 1992. Some unique aspects of pediatric fractures. In Harwood-Nash, D.C., and Pettersson, H., eds., *Pediatric radiology*. Nicer Series Merit Communications, London, 129.

83. Brogdon, B.G., and Crow, N.E. 1960. Little Leaguer's elbow. *AJR Am J Roentgenol* 83:671–75.

84. Gore, R.M., Rogers, L.F., Bowerman, J., Suker, J., and Compere, C.L. 1980. Osseous manifestations of elbow stress associated with sports activities. *AJR Am J Roentgenol* 134:971–77.

85. Bamshad, M., Van Heest, A.E., and Pleasure, D. 2009. Arthrogryposis: A review and update. *J Bone Jt Surg* 91A(Suppl. 4):40–46.

86. Guidera, K.J., Kortright, L., Barber, V., and Ogden, J.A. 1991. Radiographic changes in arthrogrypotic knees. *Skeletal Radiol* 20:193–95.

87. Fadsier, A., Wicart, P., Dubousset, J., et al. 2009. Arthrogryposis multiplex congenital. Long term follow-up from birth to skeletal maturity. *J Child Orthop* 3:383–90.

88. Larsen, L.J., and Shottstaedterbost, F.C. 1950. Multiple congenital dislocations associated with characteristic facial abnormality. *J Pediatr* 37:547–81.

89. Larville, J.M., Lakermance, P., Barber, V., and Ogden, J.A. 1994. Larsen's syndrome: Review of the literature and analysis of 38 cases. *J Pediatr Orthop* 14:63–73.

90. Gorlan, R.J., Cohen, M.M., and Levin, L.S. 1990. *Syndromes of the head and neck*, 3rd ed. New York, Oxford University Press, 722–24.

91. Steel, H.S., and Kohl, E.J. 1972. Multiple congenital dislocations associated with other skeletal anomalies (Larsen's syndrome). *J Bone Jt Surg* 54A:75–82.

92. Klenn, P.J., and Iozzo, R.V. 1991. Larsen's syndrome with novel congenital anomalies. *Hum Pathol* 22:1055–57.

93. McKusick, V.A., Francomano, C.A., Antonarakis, S.E., et al. 1994. *Mendelian inheritance in man: A catalog of human genes and genetics disorders*, 11th ed., vol. 1. Baltimore, Johns Hopkins University Press, 857–58.

94. Dich, V.Q., Nelson, J.D., and Hackett, K.C. 1975. Osteomelitis in infants and children. A review of 163 cases. *Am J Dis Child* 129:1273–78.

95. Capitanio, M.A., and Kikpatrick, J.A. 1970. Early roentgen observation in acute osteomyelitis. *AJR Am J Roentgenol* 180:488–96.

96. Taylor, M.N., Chaudhuri, R., Davis, J., Novelli, V., and Jaswon, M.S. 2008. Childhood osteomyelitis presenting as a pathological fracture. *Clin Radiol* 63:348–51.

97. King, R.W., and Johnson, D. 2009. Osteomyelitis: Differential diagnoses and workup. *Emedicine*, December 9.

98. Meschan, I. 1956. *Roentgen signs in clinical diagnosis*. Saunders, Philadelphia, 271.

99. Caffey, J., and Silverman, F.N. 1945. Infantile cortical hyperostosis: Preliminary report on a new syndrome. *AJR Am J Roentgenol* 54:1.

100. Kamoun-Goldrat, A., and Merrer, M. 2008. Infantile cortical hyperastons (Caffey disease): A review. *J Maxillofacial Surg* 66:2145–50.

101. Tien, R., Barron, B.J., and Dnenke, R.D. 1998. Caffey's disease: Nuclear case and radiologic correlation: A case of mistaken identity. *Clin Nucl Med* 13:583–85.

102. Mabiala-Babela, J.R., and Senga, P. 2005. First Congolese case report of Caffey disease. *Arch Pediatr* 12:1402.

103. Ringel, R.E., Brenner, J.I., Haney, P.J., et al. 1982. Prostaglandin-induced periostitis: A complication of long-term PGE1 infusion in an infant with congenital heart disease. *Radiology* 142:657–58.

104. Kassner, E.G. 1991. Drug-related complications in infants and children: Imaging feature. *AJR Am J Roentgenol* 157:1039–49.

105. Woo, K., Emery, J., and Peabody, J. 1994. Cortical hyperostosis following long-term prostaglandin infusion in infants awaiting cardiac transplantation. *Pediatrics* 93:417–20.

106. Letts, M., Pang, E., and Simons, J. 1994. Prostaglandin-induced neonatal periostitis. *J Pediatr Orthop* 14:809–13.

107. Rowley, R.F., and Lawson, J.P. 1991. Case report 701. *Skeletal Radiol* 20:617–19.
108. Roeper, V., and Wilderman, D., eds. 1996. *Om de noord: de tochten van Willem Braentsz en Jacob van Heemskerck en de overwintering op Nova Zembla zoals opgetekend door Gerrit de Veer.* Uitgeverji SUN, Nijmegen, The Netherlands.
109. Lips, P. 2007. Hypervitaminosis A and fractures. *Nutr Rev* 65(10):425–38.
110. Melhus, H., Michaelsson, K., Kindmark, A., et al. 1998. Excessive dietary intake of vitamin A is associated with reduced bone mineral density and increased risk for hip fractures. *Ann Intern Med* 129:770–78.
111. Feskanich, D., Singh, V., Willet, W.C., et al. 2002. Vitamin A intake and hip fractures among postmenopausal women. *JAMA* 287:47–54.
112. Caffey, J. 1972. Familial hyperphosphatasemia with ateliosis and hypermetabolism of growing membranous bone; review of the clinical, radiographic, and chemical features. *Bull Hosp Jt Dis* 33:81–110.
113. Dunn, V., Codon, V.R., and Rallison, M. 1979. Familial hyperphosphatasemia: Diagnosis in early infancy and response to human thyrocalcitonin treatment. *AJR Am J Roentgenol* 132:541–45.
114. Shopfner, C.E. 1966. Periosteal bone growth in normal infants: A preliminary report. *AJR Am J Roentgenol* 97:154–63.
115. Keats, T.E., and Anderson, M.W. 2001. *Atlas of normal roentgen variants that may simulate disease,* 7th ed. Mosby, St. Louis, 642.
116. DeSilva, P., Evans-Jones, G., Wright, A., and Henderson, R. 2003. Physiologic periostitis, a potential pitfall. *Arch Dis Child* 88:1124–25.
117. Gerald, B. 1978. Systematic radiographic evaluation of the abnormal spine. In Rabinowitz, J.G., ed., *Pediatric radiology.* Lippincott, Philadelphia, 315–18.
118. Starshak, R.J., Wells, R.G., Stry, J.R., and Gragg, D.C. 1992. *Diagnostic imaging of infants and children,* vol. II. Aspen, Gaithersburg, MD, 171–79.
119. Algra, P.R., Heimans, J.J., Valk, J., Nauta, J.J., Lachniet, M., and Van Kooten, B. 1992. Do metastases in vertebrae begin in the pedicles? Imaging study in 45 patients. *AJR Am J Roentgenol* 158:1275–79.
120. Aronica-Pollak, P.A., Stefan, V.H., and McLemore, J.M. 2003. Caronal cleft vertebra initially suspected as an abusive fracture in an infant. *J Forens Sci* 48:836–38.
121. Cohen, J., Currarino, G., and Neuhauser, E.B.D. 1956. Significant variant in the ossification centers of the vertebral bodies. *AJR Am J Roentgenol* 76:469–75.
122. Wollin, D.G., and Elliott, G.B. 1961. Caronal cleft vertebrae and persistent notochordal derivatives of infancy. *J Can Assoc Radiol* 12:78–80.
123. Crow, N.E., and Brogdon, B.G. 1959. The "normal" lumbosacral spine. *Radiology* 72:97.
124. Swischuk, L.E. 1959. *Imaging the newborn, infant and young child,* 3rd ed. Williams & Wilkins, Baltimore, 708–10.
125. Swischuk, L.E. 1970. The beaked, notched or hooked vertebra: Its significance in infants and young children. *Radiology* 95:661–68.
126. Taybi, H. 1996. Metabolic disorders. In Taybi, H., and Lachman, R.S., *Radiology of syndromes, metabolic disorders, and skeletal dysplasias,* 4th ed. Mosby, St. Louis, 670–72.
127. Kozloski, K. 1976. Metaphyseal and spondlometaphyseal chondro-dysplasias. *Clin Orthop Rel Res* 114:83–93.
128. Wynne-Davies, R., Hall, C.M., and Apley, A.G. 1985. *Atlas of skeletal dysplasias.* Churchill-Livingstone, London, 372–84.
129. Stull, M.A., Kransdor, M.J., and Devaney, K.O. 1992. Langerhans cell histiocytosis of bone. *Radiographics* 12:801–23.
130. Sanchez, T., Stewart, D., Walivich, M., Swischuk, L. 2010. Skull fractures vs. accessory sutures: How can you tell the difference? *Emerg Radiol* 17:413–18.
131. Graham, E.L. 1975. Birth trauma. *Pediatr Clin North Am* 22:317–28.

132. Barkovich, A.J. 2000. *Pediatric neuroimaging*, 3rd ed. Lippincott Williams & Wilkins, Philadelphia, 218–19.

133. Theander, G., and Theander, J. 1986. Congential deformities of skull caused by fetal limbs. *Acta Radiol (Diagn)* 21:309–13.

134. Bilo, R.A.C., Robbon, S.G., and van Rijn, R.R. 2010. *Forensic aspects of pediatric fractures.* Springer, Berlin, 22–24.

135. Hymel, K.P., and Spivack, B.S. 2001. The biomechanics of physical injury. In Reese, M., and Ludwig, S., *Child abuse: Medical diagnosis and management*, 2nd ed. Lippincott, Philadelphia, 1–22.

Credits

Brogdon, B.G., Vogel, H., and McDowell, J.D., eds., *A Radiological Atlas of Abuse, Torture, Terrorism and Inflicted Trauma*, CRC Press, Boca Raton, FL, 2002. Figures 3.2, 3.8, 3.10, 3.14, 3.15, 3.21, 3.25, 3.34a, 3.35, 3.38, 3.39b, 3.45, 3.48, 3.60, 3.62b, 3.64, 3.90.

Dermatological Signs of Physical Abuse

4

Introduction

The skin is the largest organ by area. It is the most superficial, and hence the easiest to examine. The skin is the most common presenting organ in physical child abuse. The cutaneous manifestations of physical abuse include bruises, abrasions, lacerations, swelling, burns, intraoral injuries, and human bites. Most of these examples are readily recognized by the average layperson because they are reasonably apparent. But all but one of them (the human bite) can be sustained accidentally by children capable of the required antecedent circumstances and activity.

Therefore the distinction between the accidental and nonaccidental traumatic lesion demands not only detection and analysis by an experienced, knowledgeable observer, but also careful attention to the history and overall context of the causative event.

Adding to the complexity of the diagnostic challenge is the host of the nontraumatic lesions that may mimic or suggest a traumatic etiology.

Thus the person who *by law* is forced to decide whether or not to report suspicion of physical abuse is faced with a diagnostic dilemma upon one horn of which the life of a child may hang in the balance, while upon the other depends the fragile framework of a multigenerational family.

Bruises

Bruises[1-9] are the most common signs of physical abuse, readily recognized except in heavily pigmented children. Bruises, of course, are commonly found on the normally active child. However, bruising and other soft tissue injuries are uncommon in early infancy, but increase with the increasing mobility and activity of toddlers and older children. There are patterns to consider. Normal accidental bruising is most likely over a bony prominence on the lower extremities especially, but also on the upper extremities, forehead, hips, and spine. Bruising over relatively protected areas—the upper arms, medial and posterior thighs, hands, trunk, genitalia, buttocks, cheeks, and ears—arouses suspicion of abuse (Figure 4.1), as do multiple bruises at different stages of healing or coloration. However, color alone cannot be used to estimate with accuracy the duration of time since initial injury.[1,9]

Flexibility and padding of the abdominal wall usually protects the abdomen from accidental bruising. If noted, abdominal bruising warrants investigations for internal injury. While visceral injuries are found in fewer than 5% of abusive injuries, they are highly lethal with a mortality rate of up to 50%. Thus early diagnosis is critical.[10]

Bruising of the head and face is unusual in the nonambulatory infant and the school-age child. However the unsteady gait of the toddler puts the head and face at risk (Figure 4.2). No site is immune from accidental bruising, so again, history and context, and the age and development of the child, are all important in determining causation.[7]

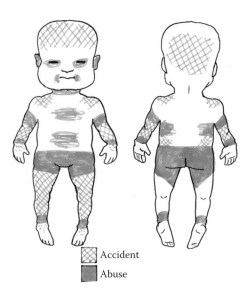

Accident

Abuse

Figure 4.1 Common anatomic sites of abusive versus accidental bruising. (Redrawn from Johnson, C.F., *Pediatr Clin North Am* 1990; 23:791–813. With permission.)

Figure 4.2 A toddler who fell against a coffee table and bruised his right forehead with resultant swelling and ecchymosis around the right eye.

The shape of a bruise can be quite helpful in determining whether a bruise was accidental or not since it may reflect the shape of the inflicting object.[1,11] Therefore patterned bruising can be a strong indication of abuse (Figure 4.3). A variety of weapons can produce linear bruises—rods, switches, wires, whips—but looped bruises are almost pathognomonic of abuse, being caused by coat hangers or doubled extension cords, ropes, or the like (Figure 4.4).

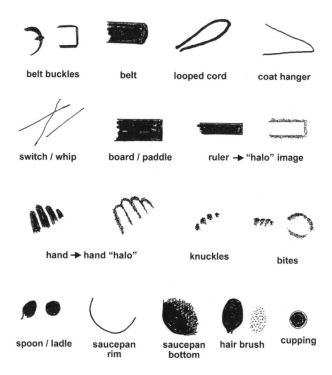

Figure 4.3 Schematic examples of pattern bruises. (Redrawn in part and expanded from Johnson, C.F., *Pediatr Clin North Am* 1990; 37:791–813. Copyright © Elsevier. With permission.)

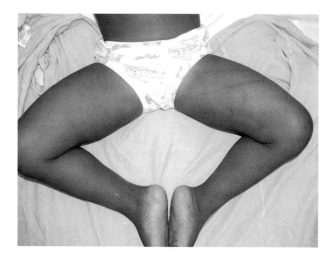

Figure 4.4 Loop marks. The grandmother, who had custody, readily admitted whipping with a coat hanger: "I was whipped by my mother, and I whipped my child and grandchild. This is how we do things!" Thus illustrating the conflicting cultural attitudes about discipline versus abuse.

The most common weapon of physical abuse is the human hand,[11] which can be used open-handed, as a fist, or as a grabber or pincher. Slapping, spanking, and grabbing often leave telltale finger marks. However, if applied at high velocity, such as a slap or whipping, the bruise may be confusing; it can appear as a "halo" or outline of the fingers or weapon rather than as a silhouette[1] (Figures 4.5 and 4.6). This is because the blood is forced laterally

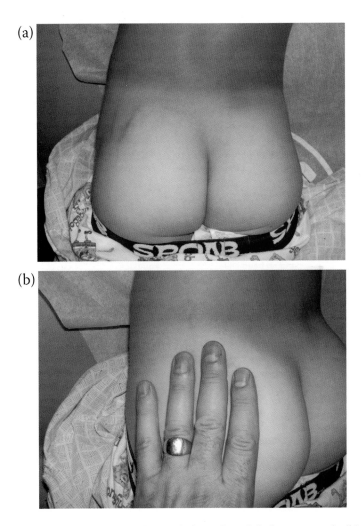

Figure 4.5 (a) Finger marks outline on buttock from forceful slap or spank. (b) Author's (T.S.) hand overlaying finger marks.

by the fingers or other narrow weapon, leaving the outline of the point of impact, which is bleached by the displacement of blood.

The upper arm is a common site for finger marks from grabbing or shaking. Binding may produce circumferential bruises around the wrist or ankles. Petechiae and edema may be evident distal to the binding site (Figure 4.1). Similar findings at the corners of the mouth can result from gagging, and at the neck from strangling (Figure 4.1).

The fist is often used against the abdomen and may produce knuckle marks. In at least one case this led to conviction of the abuser (Figure 4.7). The shoulder and upper arm is another common target for the fist, particularly in older children (Figure 4.8). Bruised eyes usually are caused by a fist in abuse (Figure 4.9). Either the fist or the open hand may be used to strike the ear. The skin over the mastoid bone behind the ear should be inspected for a bruise transmitted through the ear.[12]

Pinch-type bruises may be nonspecific in configuration, and sometimes may appear as bilobed "butterfly" marks. They are particularly suggestive of abuse if they involve the penis or female genitalia, neither of which is often injured accidentally.[13]

Figure 4.6 Two perfectly parallel lines on buttock outlining high-velocity blow from narrow flat weapon (board, ruler, paddle?).

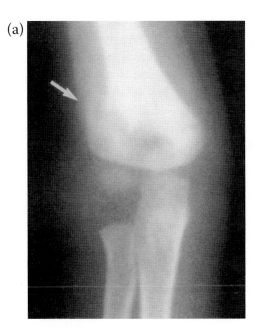

(a)

Figure 4.7 Fatal fistic blow to abdomen. (a) Baby, age 1 year, brought to ER with fresh supracondylar fracture (a bit unusual at this age).

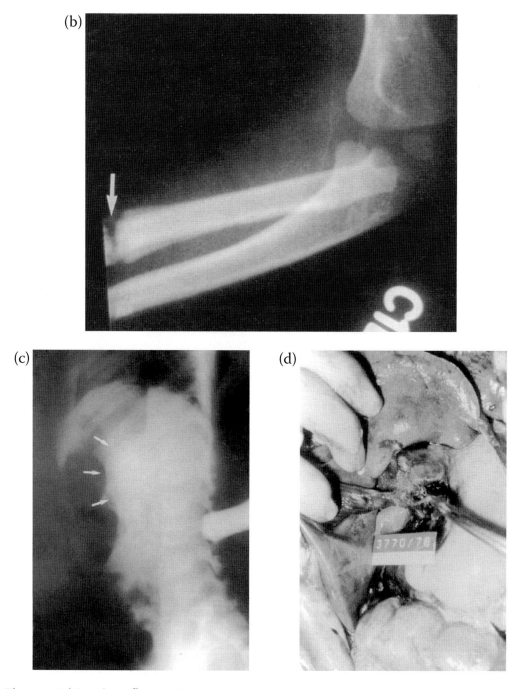

Figure 4.7 (*Continued*) Fatal fistic blow to abdomen. (b) Lateral view disclosed a second fracture of the mid-radius with nonunion. A divorce ensued with the father given custody of the abused child after he married again. The child later was returned to the ER, moribund, where a cross-table lateral of the abdomen (c) showed a large retroperitoneal mass (arrows) at autopsy. (d) Revealed laceration of the pancreas and liver and transection of the bile duct. The late Dr. James T. Westin made a cast of the stepmother's fist, which exactly matched the knuckle marks on the child's abdomen and led to a conviction. (From Brogdon, B.G., *Forensic Radiology*, 1st ed., CRC Press, Boca Raton, FL, 1998. With permission.)

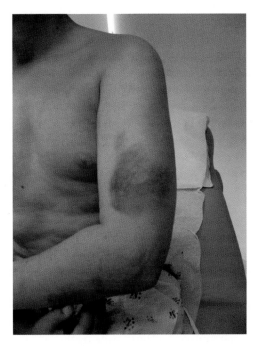

Figure 4.8 Large bruise on upper arm could be from either an aggressive or friendly blow with a fist. This turned out to be a football injury.

Figure 4.9 Black eye caused by a blow with a fist.

Abrasions and Lacerations

Abrasions and lacerations are seen in abused children but less often than bruises. Here again, the history and context of the injury is important. Accidental abrasion or laceration of the infant is unlikely. Incidence of accidental abrasions and lacerations increases with the normal development and activity of the child.

Abrasions can result from dragging the infant or young child on rough carpets or other abrasive surfaces. Weapons such as hairbrushes or combs can cause scrapes, scratches, or abrasions, as can fingernails. Fingernails digging into the flesh can cause straight or crescentic-like superficial lacerations. The edges of weapons forcefully struck may cause lacerations at the margin of the bruise.[12]

Bite Marks

Bite marks can range in appearance from faint bruising to ragged laceration, sometimes matching the dentition of the biter. Bite marks may present as a single arcuate pattern caused by a single dental arch. There may be associated "raking" of the tooth marks. A full bite will reflect both maxillary and mandibular dental arches (Figure 4.10). Penetration and laceration are most likely caused by the canine teeth.

Children bite each other at play, in anger, or in defense. A child's dental arch will be smaller than the adult dental arch, but increases with age, of course. The normal distance between the maxillary canines in the adult is 2.5–4.0 cm. There may be a relatively clear zone of skin between the bruises of the crushing injury of the bite. However, there may be sucking activity along with the bite that can fill in the space with a bruise (Figure 4.11). Sucking bruises are likely to have a sexual connotation and, along with bite marks, may have associated lacerations near the nipples or genitalia.[1,13–15]

Animal bites are quite different from human bites, tending to tear the flesh with deeper wounds, whereas human bites tend to compress superficial tissues, leaving bruising. Dogs

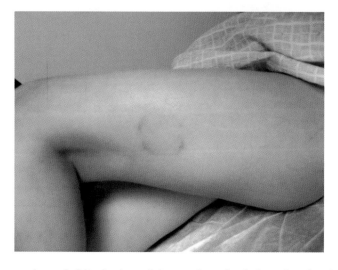

Figure 4.10 Bite mark on child's thigh with bruise from both dental arches but no laceration.

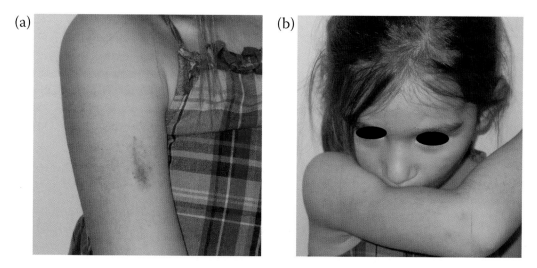

Figure 4.11 (a) Typical sucking-type bruise, suggesting the possibility of abuse with sexual connotation. (b) "Victim" shows how she produced this hickey on herself.

have a narrow mouth with prominent canines. Cat bites are small and rounded. Rodent bites have scalloped edges.[14] Photography with standard measuring devices in the field is essential for documentation of bite marks.

Hair Pulling

Forceful hair pulling is another manifestation of physical child abuse,[16,17] and can cause focal alopecia. It can be intentional as a punishing method or relatively unintentional as a parent or caretaker grabs or controls the child by the hair. Features of traumatic alopecia include petechiae at the roots of pulled hair, a boggy scalp, ragged margins, subgaleal hematoma, and acute tenderness.

Traumatic alopecia must be differentiated from alopecia areata, which usually presents with round or oval bald spots located anywhere on the scalp or other hair-bearing areas (eyebrows, lashes, or body).[17] It is thought to be of immunologic origin. There is no associated tenderness, inflammation, or pain. The involved patch is surrounded by very short hair shafts. There may be associated changes in the nails: pitting in longitudinal and transverse rows sometimes called the Scotch-plaid pattern.

Trichotillosis (also known as *trichotillomania*) is a self-inflicted traumatic alopecia caused by habitual twisting and pulling of hair, usually in children and more often in females. It results in wide swaths of missing and broken hairs, often in linear or geometric patterns in the midline or sides of the head. It usually is found on the side of the head opposite the dominant hand, thus enabling the child to continue his or her "mania" even while carrying out other tasks.[17]

Mild erythema and scaling of the scalp with partial alopecia in varying patterns is found in children with the fungal infection *tinea capitus*.[17] Commonly (and erroneously) known as ringworm of the scalp, it is not likely to be confused with traumatic hair pulling.

Burns

Burns are common among children. Up to one-third of them may be caused by physical abuse or neglect.[18] Burns in children can range from mild erythema to full-thickness dermal destruction. They are caused by hot liquids, hot objects, or burning materials with or without a flame. As with bruises, some burns have characteristic patterns. Most, however, will need evaluation of the history and circumstance, and the age, development, and activity of the child.

Burns by Hot Liquids

Burns by hot liquids result from forced immersion, or by splash burns, which can be accidental (sometimes through neglect) or purposeful. There are distinct differences and patterns of these two types.[2]

Immersion Burns

Immersion burns of an extremity usually produce striking glove or stocking-type configuration with a clear "tide mark" or demarcation line indicating the depth of immersion (Figure 4.12). However, if the child struggles against abuse, there may be coincident splash burns as well. Immersion of the body results in a different pattern. If the immersion attempt is with the baby's bottom first, flexion of the trunk and lower extremities ordinarily occurs

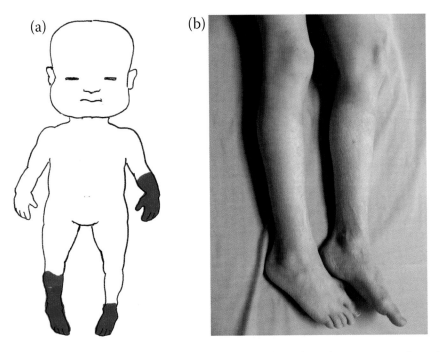

(a)   (b)

Figure 4.12 (a) Schematic drawing illustrating glove and stocking burn patterns from immersion of extremities. (b) Ten-year-old boy whose leg had been immersed in scalding water as a baby. Note the clear demarcation lines where the scarring ends at about the level of the top of "above-the-calf" stockings.

(a)

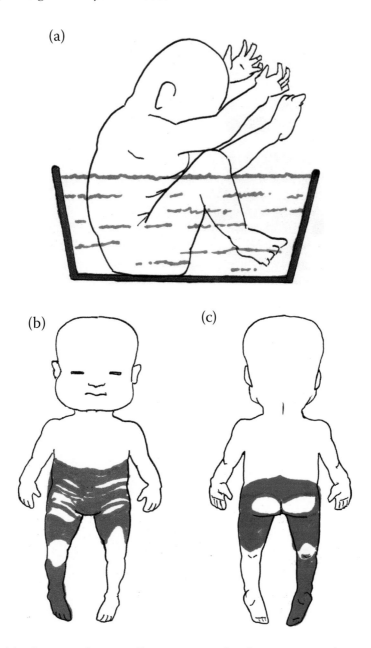

(b)   (c)

Figure 4.13 (a) Schematic drawing illustrating peculiar burn patterns that can result from bottom-first immersion of a child in a hot bath. (b) Skin folds with flexion of the trunk or extremities afford protected areas and explain the zebra-stripe pattern. (c) The "hole in the doughnut" sparing of skin pressed against the bottom of the tub.

(Figure 4.13a). In that case, there is protection of the folds of skin pressed together and burning of the exposed surfaces between folds. If we make an analogy with the brain, the gyri are burned and the sulci are spared (Figure 4.13b). If the buttocks are pressed against the bottom of the container, they are afforded protection from the surrounding hot liquid and become the "hole in the doughnut" of the surrounding burn[2,11,19,20] (Figure 4.13c).

Splash Burns

Splash burns occur when hot liquid spills onto a child. They may be abusive. Many are accidental although associated with a measure of negligence. A toddler or even a crawler can grasp an electric cord or a tablecloth and upset a torrent or hot liquid upon him- or herself. Siblings, parents, or caretakers may inadvertently spill something on the child. Context, as usual, is all-important in evaluation of accident or intent.

Splash burns in general are superficial, and cool as they are dispersed by gravity.[2,21] Consequently they are of varying depth, have irregular borders, and narrow to form tributaries of lesser severity as they spread and dissipate[3] (Figure 4.14).

Apart from burn patterns, the depth of burns attributed to hot liquids can be helpful in discrimination between accidental and abusive etiology. A child or infant with only reflex action capability will attempt to withdraw from heat. However, infantile skin can be damaged in a surprisingly short time. At the average temperature setting for residential hot water tanks, 140°F, minimal burning can occur in 3 seconds; a third-degree burn can result from as little as 15 seconds.[11] Therefore the more severe a liquid burn, the more likely it is that the body part was forcibly immersed.

Contact Burns

Contact burns can be caused by hot solids, by flaming or smoldering material, or by caustic agents, which can be liquid or solid. Contact burns also can have distinctive patterns suggestive of the causative agent (Figures 4.15–4.18). However, accidental contact burns usually are superficial and are less likely to have a distinct pattern because the body part will

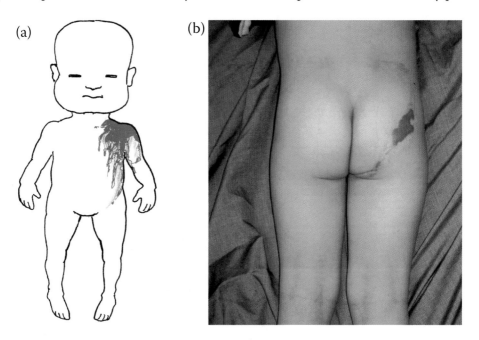

Figure 4.14 (a) Schematic drawing of a splash burn that decreases in severity from the initial contact point as it disperses. The basic pattern is an inverted triangle. (b) However, the pattern can be diverted by clothes or positioning. Hot liquid was spilled on this child at a day care center. The liquid apparently traveled along the elastic line of the diaper, cooling quickly from the initial contact point.

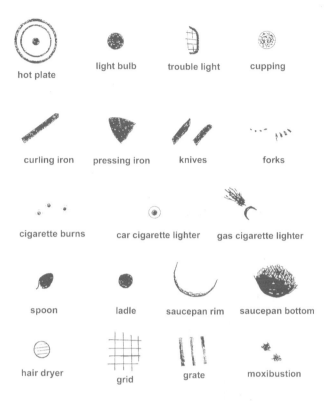

Figure 4.15 Composite schematic of patterns encountered with contact burns of varied origins. (Redrawn in part and expanded from Johnson, C.F., *Pediatr Clin North Am* 1990; 37:791–813. Copyright © Elsevier. With permission.)

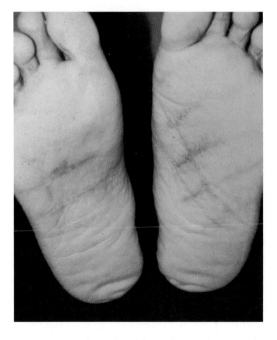

Figure 4.16 Grid pattern burns on the sole of both feet. This was from a floor furnace. Grid patterns can result from space heaters, hairdryers, grills, and shop lights.

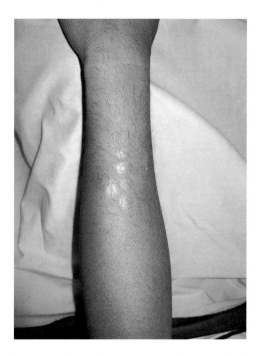

Figure 4.17 Typical uniform-sized scars from cigarette burns. The linear grouping is unusual. Hands and feet are more often involved. The victim was a disturbed teenager and the burns were self-inflicted.

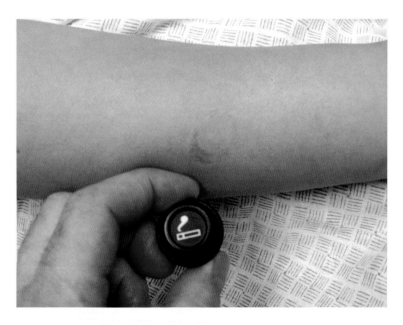

Figure 4.18 Typical pattern burn from an automobile cigarette lighter. Accidental or abusive? Depends on history, context.

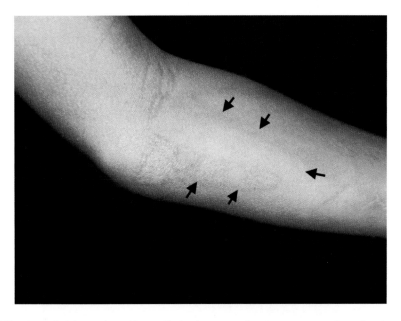

Figure 4.19 This child accidentally pulled a hot iron from an ironing board. There was only momentary contact but the pointed triangular "footprint" of the iron is faintly discernable.

be withdrawn quickly, or the hot object is accidentally brushed against only briefly, or the object strikes a glancing blow[2] (Figure 4.19).

Neither/Nor Lesions

Lesions may be occasionally encountered that are real burns, bruises, punctures, and various forms of tissue destruction, but are neither the result of normal activity nor reflective of physical abuse by others. These lesions fall into two categories: (1) self-abuse or (2) folk remedies practiced by certain ethnic or cultural groups. Although well intentioned, they produce real burns and bruises.

Personality disorders may be expressed by self-harm. The resulting damage can range from relatively innocuous to life threatening, or even unintended fatality or suicide.[22]

The sucking mark in Figure 4.11 might qualify, depending on whether this is a habitual or rhythmic behavior, which would also include the hair twisting already described, head banging, lip chewing, etc. Severe personality disorders may be expressed by minor self-mutilation, such as fine superficial incisions on the wrist or cigarette burns on the forearm, as in Figure 4.17. (The linear pattern is a giveaway; abusive burns are most often clustered on the hands and feet.[2]) These self-inflicted injuries are rarely intended to do great harm, but may become quite serious. Figure 4.20 illustrates a case of a disturbed young male who exhibited multiple puncture wounds in an upper extremity, initially thought to perhaps represent drug use. His penchant for impaling himself with wires and straightened paperclips resulted in a life-threatening situation. In Lesch-Nyhan syndrome, a metabolic disorder associated with mental retardation and excessive self-mutilation, the loss of tissue from lips, tongue, and fingers may imitate the unwitting self-mutilation of those with congenital insensitivity to pain (see Figure 3.46).

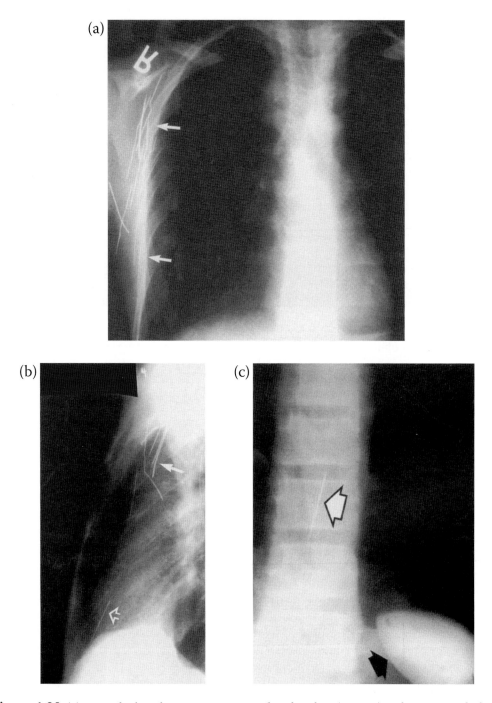

Figure 4.20 (a) Disturbed male inserts wires under the skin (arrows) in his arm and chest wall. (b, c) One wire has traveled intravenously to lodge in his right ventricle (open arrow on lateral view, white arrow on frontal view). He also swallows foreign objects (black arrow points to large foreign body in the gastric fundus). Location of the insertions clearly indicates that the subject is left-handed.

Cultural Remedies, Folk Medicine

Several treatment methods derived from our multicultural population can be confused with physical abuse.[1,2,11,23,24] It is important to recognize these because accusations of abuse based on these ancient remedies can be devastating to those who practice them in good faith. At least one suicide has been reported in a Vietnamese man so accused by authorities unfamiliar with a procedure common in that ethnic group.[25]

Coining

Variations of coining are found in many cultures. Generally, it is a procedure of rubbing a hard object upon skin (frequently oiled beforehand) in patterns on the back or occasionally the forehead. It is believed by its practitioners and patients to reduce fever, and especially to treat the common cold. In China, it is called *gua sha*, which translates as "to scrape away fever." The rubbing tool may be a porcelain soup spoon, horn, bone, or jade. In Indonesia it is known as Kerikan. The large immigration into the United States and Canada in the 1970s from Southeast Asia has spread *cao gio* (Vietnamese for "to scrape wind"), widely practiced, particularly in fishing villages along our coastlines. The common tool is the edge of a coin or a spoon. Patterned bruises resembling a "stick figure" tree are the usual result[26] (Figures 4.21 and 4.22).

Cupping

Cupping is found mostly in Latin American and Russian populations. A glass cup is heated by placing a lighted candle inside or by coating the inside of the glass with alcohol and

(a) 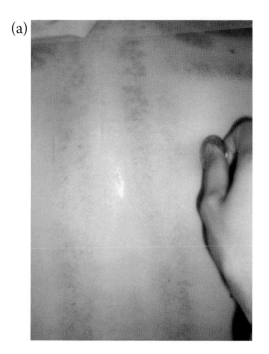 (b)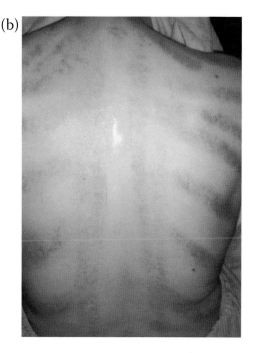

Figure 4.21 (a) Cao gio (coining) being practiced on the Alabama Gulf Coast using the edge of a coin to produce (b) a symmetrical tree pattern on the back. (Courtesy Brandon Nichols, MD.)

(a)

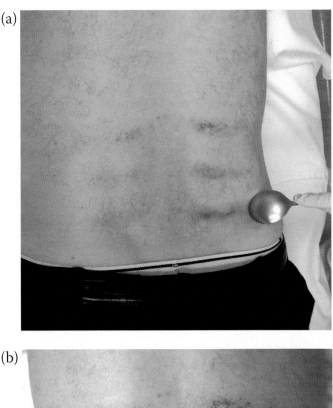

(b)

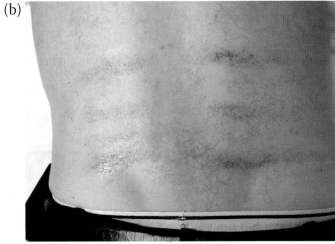

Figure 4.22 (a) Spooning in Detroit with... (b) a slightly different tree pattern.

igniting it. It is then placed upon the back, and as the glass cools a vacuum is formed. After the glass is removed, an imprint of its rim remains and is subsequently filled in by a circle of erythematous skin.[23] A modern variation uses a suction device to create the vacuum without heat (Figure 4.23).

Moxibustion

Moxibustion apparently originated in ancient China. A native herb, AiYe (Moxa), which we know as mugwort, is burned to strengthen the blood or blood flow and to maintain

(a)

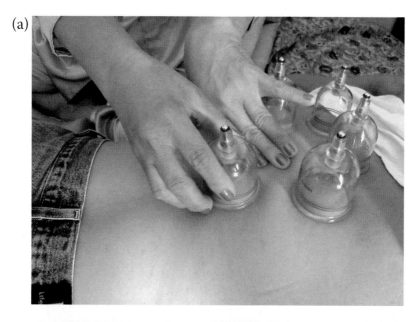

(b)

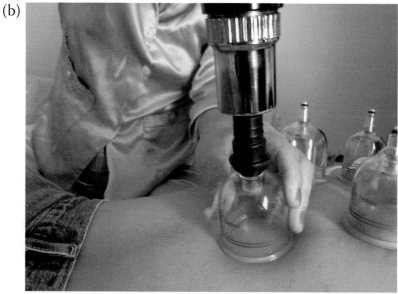

Figure 4.23 Cupping. (a) Glass cups are placed on the back. (b) A suction device produces a vacuum without the necessity for heat.

(c)

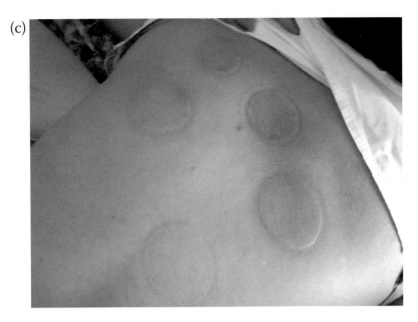

Figure 4.23 (*Continued*) Cupping. (c) The desired lesion is produced upon removal of the glass.

(a)

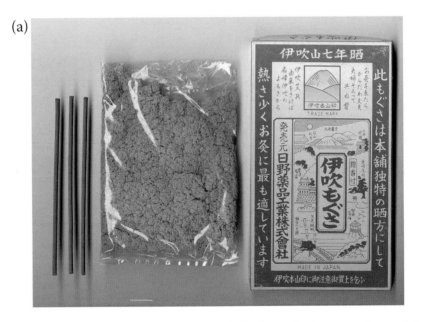

Figure 4.24 Moxibustion. (a) Ibuki moxa set available from the Internet. On the left are the moxa "cigars," which can be separately purchased online; a box of 10 costs $8.95. In the middle package is bulk moxa for shaping into balls for skin application. Cardboard box on the right.

(b)

(c)

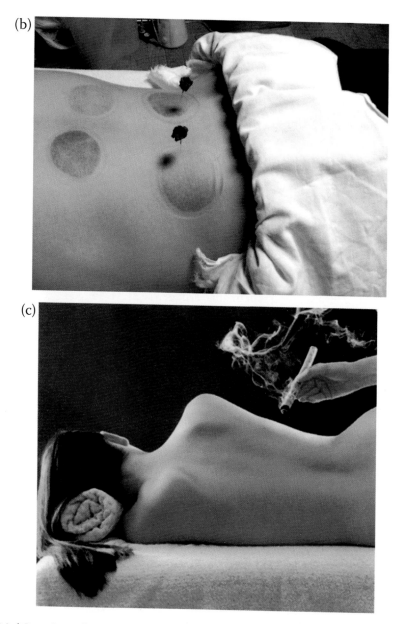

Figure 4.24 (Continued) Moxibustion. (b) Combination therapy: Cupping, surface moxibustion, and (at top) moxa on an acupuncture needle. (From Wikipedia, not copyrighted.) (c) Commercial advertisement on the Internet (Google) showing use of the moxa cigar.

general health.[24,26] Several methods are employed: (1) The moxa is wadded into small balls, placed on the skin and ignited; (2) it is placed on small dishes on the skin before ignition; (3) the moxa is rolled into a tubular shape resembling a cigar in size and shape, ignited, and held close to the skin as it smolders to produce erythema; or (4) it is combined with acupuncture by placing the moxa atop the acupuncture needle, which then carries the heat of the smoldering moxa into deeper tissues (Figure 4.24).

Caida de la Mollera

Caida de la mollera comes from Mexico as a "sunken fontanelle," which is recognized in Western medicine as usually a sign of dehydration. Caida de la mollera is treated by pushing upwards on the palate, rubbing the margins of the fontanelle, applying a raw egg to the fontanelle, or hanging the child upside down. This latter treatment has been accused of replicating some of the findings in shaken baby syndrome, namely retinal and intracranial hemorrhages,[27] although at least one paper rejects this indictment.[28]

References

1. Kors, L., and Shwayder, T. 2006. Cutaneous manifestations of child abuse. *Pediatr Dermatol* 23:311–20.
2. Lane, W. 2003. Diagnosis and management of physical abuse in children. *Clin Fam Pract* 5:493–514.
3. Pressel, D.M. 2000. Evaluation of physical abuse in children. *Am Fam Physician* 61:3057–64.
4. Coulter, K. 2000. Bruising and skin trauma. *Pediatr Rev* 21:34–35.
5. Chadwick, D.L. 1992. The diagnosis of inflicted injury in infants and young children. *Pediatr Ann* 21:477–83.
6. Sugar, N.F., Taylor, J.A., and Feldman, K.W. 1999. Bruises in infants and toddlers: Those who don't cruise rarely bruise. Puget Sound Pediatric Research Network. *Arch Pediatr Adolesc Med* 153:399–403.
7. Carpenter, R.F. 1999. The prevalence and distribution of bruising in babies. *Arch Dis Child* 80:363–66.
8. Pascoe, J.M., Hildebrandt, H.M., Tarrier, A., and Murphy, M. 1979. Patterns of skin injury in nonaccidental and accidental injury. *Pediatrics* 64:245–47.
9. Maguire, S., Mann, M.K., Sibert, J., and Kemp, A. 2005. Are there patterns of bruising in childhood which are diagnostic or suggestive of abuse? A systematic review. *Arch Dis Child* 90:182–86.
10. Lonergan, G.J., Baker, A.M., Morey, M.K., and Boos, S.C. 2003. Child abuse: Radiographic-pathologic correlation. *Radiographics* 23:811–45.
11. Johnson, C.F. 1990. Inflicted injury versus accidental injury. *Pediatr Clin North Am* 23:791–813.
12. Zitelli, B.J., and Davis, H.W. 2007. *Atlas of pediatric physical dignosis*, 5th ed. Mosby, Philadelphia, 169.
13. Raimer, B.G., Raimer, S.S., and Hebeler, J.R. 1981. Cutaneous signs of child abuse. *J Am Acad Dermatol* 5:203–14.
14. Wagner, G.N. 1986. Bitemark identification in child abuse cases. *Pediatr Dent* 8:96–100.
15. McDowell, J.D. 2004. Role of the health professional in diagnosing pattern injuries from birth to death. In Dorian, R.B.J., ed., *Bitemark evidence*. CRC Press, Boca Raton, FL, 25–31.
16. Hamlin, H. 1968. Subgaleal hematoma caused by hair-pull. *JAMA* 204:129.
17. Zitelli, B.J., and Davis, H.W. *Atlas of pediatric physical diagnosis*, 5th ed. Mosby, Philadelphia, 2007, 337–42.
18. Jenny, C. 2001. Cutaneous manifestations of child abuse. In Reece, R.M., and Ludury, S., eds., *Child abuse: Medical diagnosis and management*. Lippincott Williams & Wilkins, Philadelphia, 23–45.
19. Hobbs, C.J. 1986. When are burns not accidental? *Arch Dis Child* 61:357–61.
20. Stratman E, Meloki J. 2002. Scold abuse. *Arch Dermatol* 138:318–20.
21. Purdue, G.F., Hunt, J.L., and Perscott, P.R. 1988. Child abuse by burning: An index of suspicion. *J Trauma* 28:221–14.
22. Putnam, N., and Stein, M. 1985. Self-inflicted injuries in childhood: A review and diagnostic approach. *Clin Pediatr* 24:514–18.

23. Asnes, R.S., and Wisotsky, D.H. 1981. Cupping lesions simulating child abuse. *J Pediatr* 99:267–28.
24. Reinhart, M.A., and Ruhs, H. 1985. Moxibustion. Another traumatic folk remedy. *Clin Pediatr* 24:58–59.
25. Chin, W.Y. 2005. Blue spots, coining, and cupping: How ethnic minority parents can be misreported as child abusers. *J Law Soc* 7:88–115.
26. Wikipedia. 2011. Cultural remedies/folk medicine.
27. Guarnaschelli, J., Lee, J., and Pitts, F.W. 1972. Fallen fontanelli: A variant of the shaken baby syndrome. *JAMA* 222:1545–46.
28. Hansen, K.K. 1997. Folk remedies and child abuse: A review with emphasis on caida de mollera and its relationship to the shaken baby syndrome. *Child Abuse Negl* 22:217–27.

Dermatological Mimics of Physical Abuse

5

Introduction

Chapters 2 and 4 have shown that there are certain patterns, locations, and appearances (whether visual or radiological) that arouse suspicion of nonaccidental injury. These suspicions may be reinforced or allayed by the history and total context of the traumatic incident, including timing of seeking medical attention, consistency of history, age and development of the child, social and family history, and caretaker's concern.

The cutaneous indications of trauma are more or less obvious depending on location, and pigmentation of the child in question. As previously shown, dermatological lesions of accidental trauma tend to be small, few in number, nonspecific in configuration, and mostly restricted to certain locations (Figures 4.3 and 4.12–4.15).

Although the cutaneous manifestations of physical trauma are relatively few—bruises, burns, abrasions, scars, scratches, lacerations—a rather amazing, sometimes daunting, array of nontraumatic dermatological conditions may be confused with one of those traumatic categories[1-9] (Table 5.1). Some are commonplace and may be recognizable by many in the general population. Others are uncommon even in dermatological practice and relatively unfamiliar to most health care or social workers. To include discussion and illustration of all of those mimics is beyond the scope and capability of this small volume. Exemplars of nontraumatic conditions simulating the range of abusive skin lesions are presented to emphasize the problems of differentiating accidental from nonaccidental trauma, and trauma from nontrauma, in infants and children, and the necessity for consideration of context in every case.

Two excellent resources are available on the Internet for anyone who wishes to investigate the visual manifestation of any dermatological condition: DermAtlas offers almost 13,000 full-color images of skin lesions, and almost 7,000 images of affectations in the pediatric age group. These have been collected by dermatologists at Johns Hopkins University in Baltimore, Maryland, for the benefit of all health care professionals. Of equal quality are 1,300 topics provided on DermNet NZ, the website of the New Zealand Dermatological Society.

Mimics of Bruises

The most common visible lesion of accidental trauma is the bruise, well recognized by almost everyone. However, an array of nontraumatic dermatological conditions can produce somewhat similar areas of discoloration of the skin. Differentiation and diagnosis of the mimicking lesions may be difficult.

Hyperpigmentation

Mongolian spots are patchy areas of hyperpigmentation commonly found in infants of African, Mediterranean, and Asian descent. They are caused by collections of increased

Table 5.1   Dermatological Conditions That May Mimic Physical Abuse[1–9]

As Bruises	As Scratches, Scrapes, Scars, Lacerations	As Burns
Disseminated intravascular coagulation (DIC)	Amniotic bands	Bullous mastocytosis
Ehlers-Danlos dermatorhexis	Insect bites/stings	Cat-scratch fever
Erythema multiforme	Koebner phenomenon	Discoid lupus erythematosis
Erythema nosodum	Linear IgA dermatitis	Disseminated lupus erythematosis
Hemophilia	Morphea (en coup de sabre)	Epidermolysis bullosa
Hypersensitivity vasculitis	Staphylococcal scalded skin syndrome (SSSS)	Fixed drug eruption
Idiopathic thrombocytopenia	Striae	Immunoincompetence
Lichen aureus		Impetigo
Lichen sclerosis et atrophicus		Junctional epidermolysis bullosa
Mongolian spots		Laxative-induced dermatitis
Morphea		Linear IgA dermatitis
Phytophotodermatitis		Morphea
Pityriasis rosea		Pityriasis lichenoides
Platelet aggregation disorder		Pityriasis rosea
Postinflammatory hyperpigmentation		Pityriasis rubra
Purpura fulminans of meningococcemia		Pityriasis rubra pilaris
Pyoderma gangrenosum		Ringworm (tinea)
Salicylate poisoning		Seborrheic dermatitis
Schönlein-Henoch purpura		Schamberg's pupura
Vitamin K deficiency		Staphylococcal scalded skin syndrome (SSSS)
von Willebrandt's disease		Toxic epidermoid necrosis

amounts of melanin in the epidermis and can be mistaken for bruises. Most often found over the sacral region and buttocks, they can also be present in other areas. They are asymptomatic, of no clinical significance, and will disappear during the first years of life[7,8] (Figure 5.1a).

Postinflammatory hyperpigmentation may appear following the acute phase of an inflammatory exanthem, especially in children with dark skin. They are nontender, do not change in color in a few days as bruises do, and of course, the history of the previous inflammation reveals the true nature of the lesions[8] (Figure 5.1b).

Purpura

Purpura is the collective term for a group of disorders characterized by purplish or brownish red discoloration easily visualized through the epidermal layers of the skin. It is caused by hemorrhage into underlying tissue by a number of clinical entities with a wide variety of etiologies and subtypes. Not all purpural diseases mimic bruises. As will be shown, other traumatic skin lesions can be simulated by the so-called purpural diseases at some stage of their development or regression.

(a) 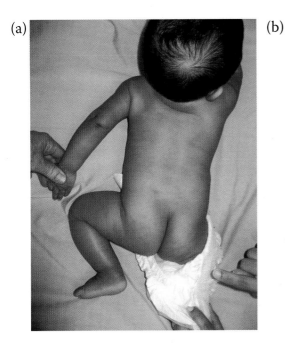 (b)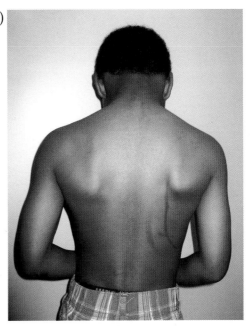

Figure 5.1 (a) Congenital hyperpigmentation. Mongolian Spots in the most common location over the sacrum and the buttocks. The extensive involvement of the left upper extremity is unusual (Indian infant). (b) Acquired hyperpigmentation. This 6-year-old African-American male, playing in the woods, stood up suddenly under a pine tree and scratched his back against the rough bark. Postinflammatory hyperpigmentation along the course of the healing scratches could be mistaken for bruises from a beating. Given the symmetrical arrangement of the markings, intentional bruising such as coining could be considered.

It must be remembered that children with disorders causing purpura or other cutaneous lesions mimicking physical trauma can also be victims of abuse, so history and context remain all-important in the total evaluation of these children.

Schönlein-Henoch purpura is the most common vasculitis affecting children.[8,9] It is often found after the affected child has had a viral or streptococcal infection. It usually appears first as purpura below the waist accompanied with or preceded by arthralgia, abdominal pain, and hematuria. The size and configuration of the lesions are variable and can progress to plaques, vesicles, or even necrosis. Knowledge of the history and the usual course and evolution of the lesions will help prevent misdiagnosis, but traumatic lesions can be closely resembled at times (Figures 5.2 and 5.3).

Lichen Aureus

Lichen aureus is a subtle capillaritis. The deposition of hemoglobin breakdown products in the skin can be mistaken for bruising. It often is asymmetrical. Here, the pattern on the left buttock greatly resembles "halo" marks from a paddle or ruler (Figure 5.4).

Erythema Nodosum

Erythema nodosum is characterized by tender, reddened nodular lesions situated on the legs between knees and ankles. It is more or less convincingly related to or associated with a

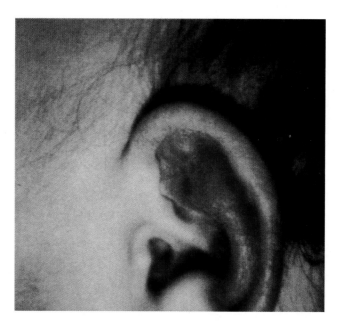

Figure 5.2 Schönlein-Henoch purpura involving the ear of a child. This could easily be the result of an abusive blow, but in that case, one might expect a transmitted bruise over the mastoid process behind the ear.

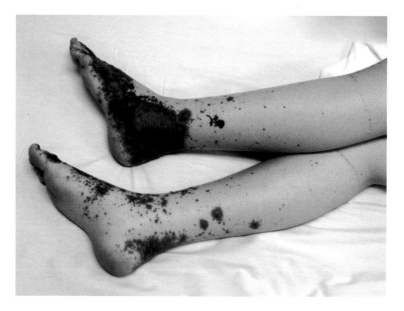

Figure 5.3 Schönlein-Henoch purpura can be quite dramatic in appearance and distribution, with hemorrhagic bullae scattered upon the deep red background.

broad spectrum of infectious diseases, usually of a chronic nature. It is thought most likely to represent a hypersensitivity reaction to the concurrent infection. Occasionally drugs are thought to provoke the reaction. However, no cause can be found for many outbreaks.

The individual lesions, 1–5 cm in diameter, can resemble bruises, but the location and multiplicity of the lesions and the disclosure of a coexisting chronic infection will dispel suspicions of abuse[10,11] (Figure 5.5).

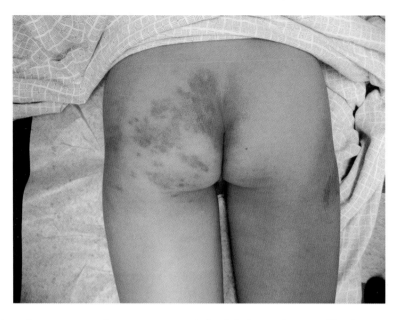

Figure 5.4 Lichen aureus. The appearance of the left buttock resembles bruising with halo outlines suggesting two blows with a ruler or paddle.

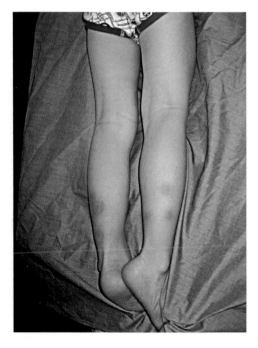

Figure 5.5 Erythema nodosum. Typical red nodules on the legs that could reflect several blows with a small weapon. The multiplicity and location of the lesions argue against that, and the finding of an associated chronic infection will confirm the correct diagnosis.

Morphea

Morphea or localized scleroderma is a rare disease of childhood with an estimated incidence of 0.02–0.04/100,000.[12] There are five subtypes: plaque morphea, generalized morphea, linear morphea or linear scleroderma, bullous morphea, and deep morphea.[13] Although rare, morphea is a great imitator and in its various forms can suggest virtually all of the cutaneous presentations of physical abuse.[13–16]

Early active lesions frequently present with a "herald" patch characterized by a violaceous inflammatory border surrounding fibrosis confined to the skin, subcutaneous tissue, or muscle. It may present as plaques or drops ("guttate" morphea), diffuse cutaneous involvement, or linear sclerosis involving a single dermatome, and can cause severe deformity and growth disturbances in a limb. When a deep linear lesion occurs on the scalp or face, it can be quite disfiguring (Figures 5.6–5.10).

If no growth arrest or disfigurement has occurred in the milder forms, spontaneous recovery may occur in children.

Fixed Drug Eruption

All physicians and most of the general public are aware that cutaneous reactions can be caused by a wide variety of internal and external agents, including drugs taken for therapeutic purposes. Most trigger a generalized reaction of patches, plaques, nodules, or vesicles spreading widely over most of the body.

Fixed drug eruptions describe a phenomenon wherein a cutaneous drug reaction occurring in a given site with the initial insult will recur in the same location upon a repeated dose of the offending agent. Additional sites may respond to a subsequent provocation, but the original site will flare up again. Bruises, burns, or blisters can be simulated by fixed drug eruption[17] (Figures 5.11–5.13).

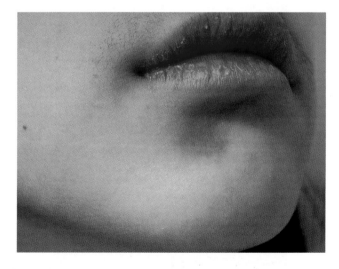

Figure 5.6 Morphea. This 11-year-old girl presented with a reddish gray mark on her lower lip and chin that could be compared to the blow to the chin seen frequently in abuse of intimate partners.[17] However, rather than being swollen, this area is depressed and has been slowly evolving for weeks.

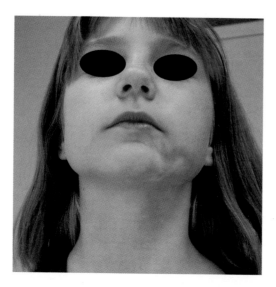

Figure 5.7 Morphea can be easily mistaken for an old burn. The area on this 8-year-old girl's jaw appears as broad and reddish, with a depressed, widened, linear scar-like center.

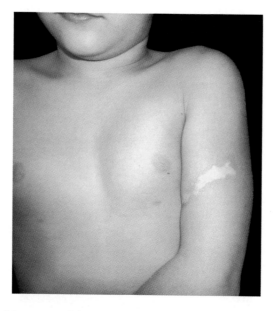

Figure 5.8 Morphea. A burn-scar-like patch on the arm of this 9-year-old boy.

Pityriasis Rosea

Pityriasis rosea is a generalized, rather benign rash commonly appearing in adolescent children and young adults. It may have mild prodromal constitutional symptoms. The first cutaneous lesion is a herald patch usually on the trunk, a large oval pink lesion with a slightly scaly center. It sometimes resembles tinea corporis (common ringworm).[18] The herald lesion can be confusing until the more generalized eruption appears (Figure 5.14).

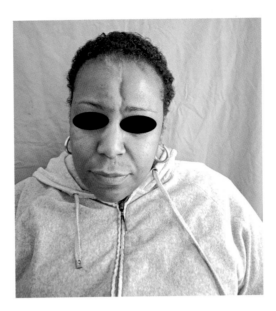

Figure 5.9 Morphea (en coup de sabre). This terrible deformity on the face and forehead of a 43-year-old female has been present since early childhood. It appears to be the result of a blow with an edged weapon (i.e., a saber or axe). The off-center location on the brow is typical. This type of deep linear scleroderma can distort and destroy underlying bone, deform the orbit, and rearrange the maxilla and teeth.

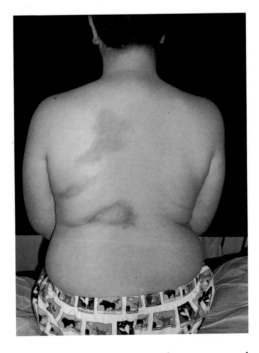

Figure 5.10 Morphea. The back of this youngster demonstrates the versatility of localized scleroderma. The large discoloration adjacent to the medial border of the left scapula suggests a bruise. The parallel stripes over the left posterolateral rib cage resemble marks from a beating (or even localized coining in an unusual direction). The multicolored lesion to the left of the mid-back could be an aging bruise.

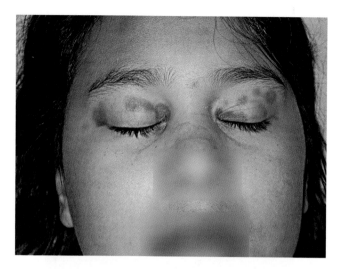

Figure 5.11 Fixed drug eruption on the eyelids of this young female look like fading black eyes from physical violence.

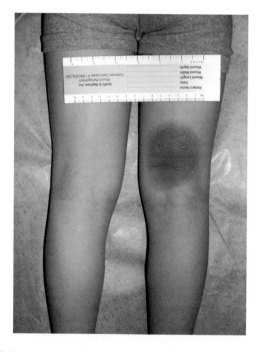

Figure 5.12 This fixed drug eruption in a peculiar location could represent a contact burn or a "grab" bruise.

Pyoderma Gangrenosum

Pyoderma gangrenosum comes on as a red, hot plaque that often breaks down into rapidly advancing ulcers. The distribution can be quite irregular and asymmetrical. Particularly in the early phase before ulceration, the lesions can be mistaken for many things, including abuse (Figure 5.15). Fortunately, pyoderma gangrenosum is uncommon in children and rare in infancy. It often can be associated with chronic diseases (i.e., ulcerative colitis) in

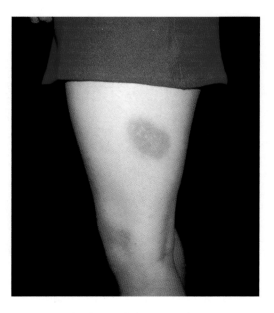

Figure 5.13 Fixed drug eruption of color and shape conforming to a pattern similar to a blow with a large spoon or ladle—maybe even a hot spoon or ladle.

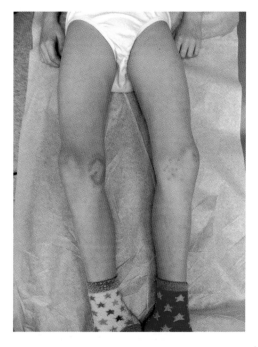

Figure 5.14 Pityriasis rosea. Although the herald lesion can appear anywhere, this large one on the knee could be confused by an inexperienced observer with abuse.

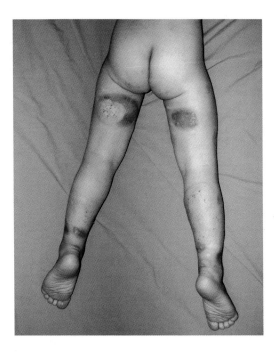

Figure 5.15 Pyoderma gangrenosum in a 2-year-old child. The early lesions can be confusing. For instance, the markings on the inner and posterior surfaces of the proximal thighs could be mistaken for grab marks associated with sexual assault, or first and second degree burns. The circumferential bands at the ankles somewhat resemble binding marks, but there is no distal edema or petechiae.

adults, and less commonly in children.[19] The dreadful appearance of the full-blown flesh-eating ulceration (Figure 5.16) is diagnosed by biopsy of its leading edge.

Lichen Sclerosis et Atrophicus

This condition is found most often in the urogenital area in both sexes, but the female-to-male ratio is 6:1. Children make up about 15% of cases.[20] In young girls the onset may be associated with pruritis, burning, vaginal discharge, and erythema, which along with scratching and bruising can resemble sexual abuse (Figure 5.17). Later the lesions become less erythematous and more porcelain colored, and coalesce into a plaque-like formation in the urogenital area.

In boys the condition often causes phimosis and is the most common cause for post-neonatal circumcision.

This is common in patients with morphea.

Mimics of Other Pattern Injuries

Amniotic Bands

Amniotic band syndrome is a rare condition thought to result from tears in the amniotic sac. Fibrous bands form (perhaps in conjunction with the chorionic mesenchyme) that float about in the amniotic fluid and may attach to or encircle fetal parts.[21,22] Three categories of injury can occur: visceral defects, craniofacial defects (mostly in the form of clefts),

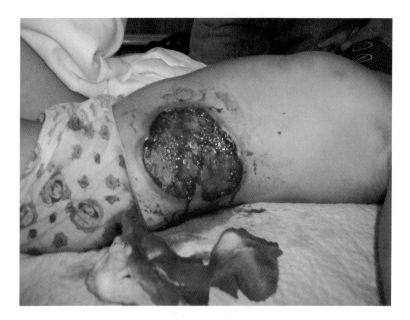

Figure 5.16 Pyoderma granulosum with advanced large ulcer in a 5-year-old female.

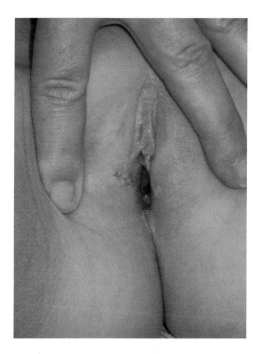

Figure 5.17 Lichen sclerosis et atrophicus. Typical appearance and location in a 10-year-old female. Sexual abuse could be suspected.

and limb defects. The latter can range from small soft tissue indentation to total amputation or absence of the limb distal to the encircling band.

Minimal indentations can resemble scars from whip marks or constricting ligatures or restraints (Figure 5.18). Circumferential bands with minimal compression can cause soft tissue swelling distally (congenital lymphedema).

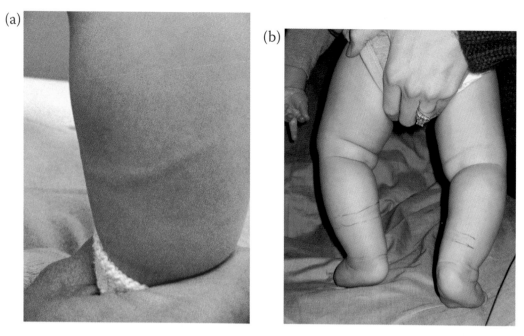

Figure 5.18 Amniotic bands. (a) A furrow across the lower limb of an infant is probably related to an amniotic band. It could suggest a scar of unknown origin or a whip mark. (b) There are fairly deep partial indentations on the left lower thigh. On the right there is more of an encircling compression ring with minimal distal swelling (congenital lymphedema). There are no distal petechiae or discolorations to suggest postnatal binding.

Striae

Physiologic striae, or "stretch marks," are thin lines or bands of reddened skin (which later become white, smooth, shiny, and depressed) on the back, buttocks, breasts, and abdomen. They occur in about 5% of adolescent children between ages 12 and 16. These livid stripes can be mistaken for whip marks or, later, as residual scars from lashings. They can result from rapid growth or weight gain, pregnancy, endocrine and connective tissue disorders, and steroid therapy. As usual, a careful history will usually dispel the suspicion of abuse[23] (Figure 5.19).

Staphylococcal Scalded Skin Syndrome (SSSS)

Staphylococcal scalded skin syndrome (SSSS) will be illustrated again later as it is most often confused with burns. It also is confused with erythema multiforme in some manifestations.[24] It is an exfoliating epidermal necrosis typically following an erythematous cellulitis caused by toxins from some strains of *Staphylococcus aureus*.

Severity of involvement can vary from superficial blistering to extreme exfoliation of skin involving almost the entire body.[25] The exfoliative patterns can simulate different types of traumatic injury, whether accidental or intentionally inflicted (Figure 5.20).

Koebner Phenomenon

Named for a nineteenth-century German dermatologist, Koebner phenomenon refers to skin lesions that appear on lines of trauma, that trauma most often being only the

(a)   (b)

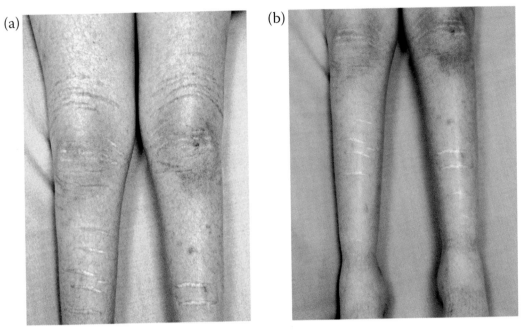

Figure 5.19 (a) Striae in reddish parallel bands above the knees and lower shins resembling whip marks. This teenager suffered from Burkett's lymphoma and had received massive doses of steroids. (b) Older striae on the anterior legs have become white and shiny but could be suspected as scars from a whipping.

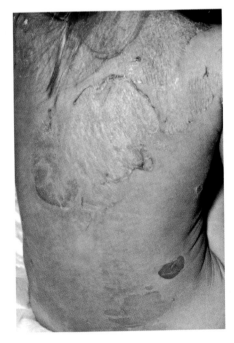

Figure 5.20 Staphylococcal scalded skin syndrome in a young boy. The oval patch on the right flank looks like a burn. The margins of the broad, rather superficial exfoliation on the back at first glance resemble marks from a looped whip.

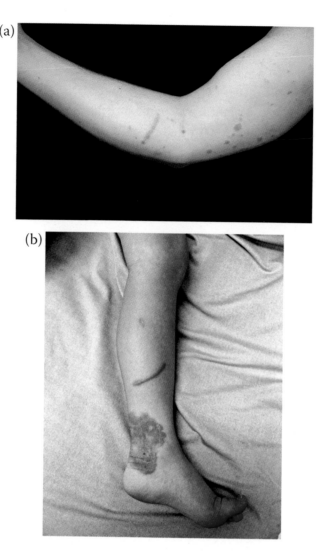

Figure 5.21 (a) Koebner reaction or phenomenon in a 17-year-old male with psoriasis, here manifested by a few of the small reddish raised nodules seen more often in young patients.[26] Two large red linear Koebner reactions could be confused with whip marks or abusive scratches. (b) Four-year-old with Well's syndrome,[27] an eosinophilic cellulitis with pruritic rashes or plaque, sometimes vesicles and bullae, of unknown cause. The primary lesion is at the ankle. An angry-looking Koebner reaction could be easily mistaken for an abusive lesion.

simple act of scratching oneself where it itches! Quite reasonably, it is seen in persons already suffering from some pruritic affliction, psoriasis being the most common. With "Koebnerization" new lesions of the preexisting condition appear where the skin is injured (scratched, rubbed, pierced) (Figure 5.21).

Burns

As discussed in Chapter 4, burns can result from contact with a hot surface or flame, immersion or splashing with hot liquids, or contact with caustics or irritants of various sorts. Nontraumatic dermatological conditions can resemble all of these thermal or caustic injuries. Examples of these mimicking conditions ranging over that spectrum are presented here.

Lupus Erythematosis

Systemic lupus erythematosis is the most common rheumatic disease of children with significant morbidity and mortality.[28] The disease is photosensitive, so the erythema presents in exposed areas of the skin. Arthritis, arthralgias, and Reynaud's phenomenon are common presenting symptoms. Multiple organ systems may eventually be involved (Figure 5.22).

Discoid lupus erythematosis is rare in children. Initial location on the face is predominant. The lesions are small, rounded, and erythematous, then become scaly and hyperpigmented.[28] They can look quite like a healing cigarette burn (Figure 5.23).

Schamberg's Purpura

Schamberg's disease is an apparently innocuous and common type of capillaritis with crops of reddish brown patches with cayenne pepper spots on the borders from hemoglobin leaked from intradermal capillaries. It is asymptomatic. Size and distribution of the lesions are quite variable. Isolated small round crops can simulate traumatic abusive lesions[29,30] (Figure 5.24).

Pityriasis Lichenoides

Pityriasis lichenoides is of unknown etiology and embraces a broad spectrum of presentations, from acute papules to pseudovesicles to small scaling papules.[31] Lesions appear in crops. The pustular variant resembles crops of impetigo, and thus cigarette burns (Figure 5.25).

Linear IgA Dermatitis

This disease is characterized by vesicles and bullae that can occur anywhere, but may group and blister in arciform patterns sometimes referred to as "a string of pearls." The

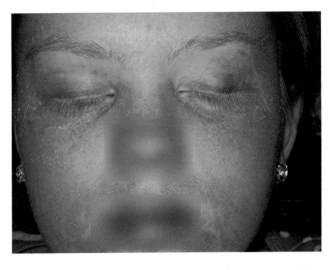

Figure 5.22 Acute lupus erythematosis. This young teenager with diffuse facial erythema might be thought the victim of a negligent sunburn or overexposure in a tanning bed, but she has the typical malar rash of acute systemic lupus erythematosis.

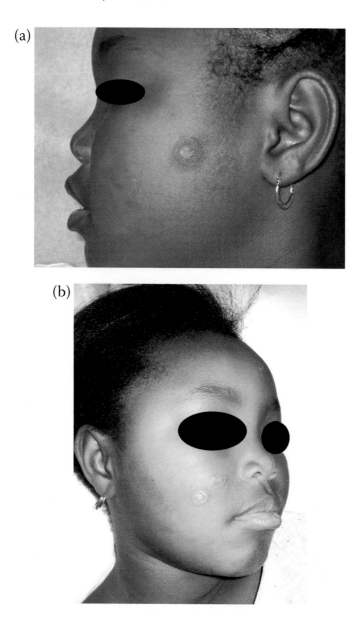

Figure 5.23 (a, b) Discoid lupus erythematosis. Two girls, 8½ and 9 years old, have almost identical facial lesions resembling healing cigarette burns.

lesions itch, and with scratching may bleed. In appearance and location, such as the case illustrated here, suspicion of abuse is easily aroused. Acute onset of bullae in the groin (Figure 5.26) is rare.

Bullous Mastocytosis

Cutaneous mastocytosis in children may present as urticaria pigmentosa, many small reddish brown papules, or plaques that may develop small vesicles or bullae resembling burns (Figure 5.27). They are most often located on the trunk and simulate burns. Cutaneous

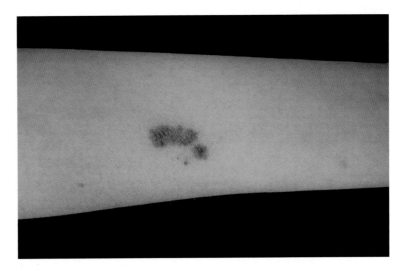

Figure 5.24 Schamberg's disease or purpura in a 12-year-old male shows a close collection of rounded lesions that could suggest a series of contact burns. In this case the inexperienced observers might even consider a raking bite mark from a maxillary arch. If this condition, however benign, provokes enough concern, biopsy is required to confirm the diagnosis.

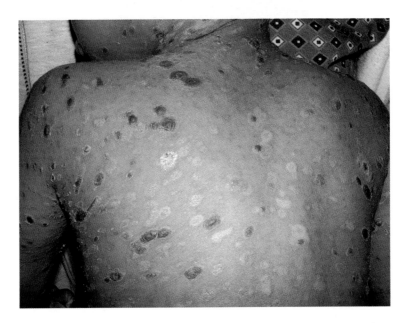

Figure 5.25 Pityriasis lichenoides et varioliformis acuta (PLEVA) in a young African-American male. Multiple vesicles and crusts simulate cigarette burns.

mastocytosis can be present at birth and may resolve in adolescence. It may be accompanied by the interesting finding of dermatographia.[32]

Pityriasis Rubra

This common condition sometimes has an exuberant herald patch that can be mistaken for a burn (Figure 5.28).

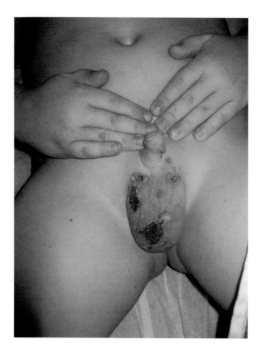

Figure 5.26 Linear IgA bullous dermatosis in a 6-year-old with bruising, bleeding, and crusting scrotal lesions suggests the possibility of bruising pinches, sexual abuse.

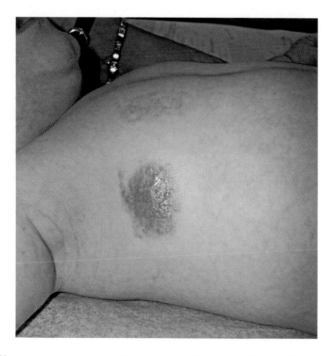

Figure 5.27 Bullous mastocytosis on the chest of a 7-week-old baby. This discrete area of mild blistering recurred multiple times. It looks like a second-degree burn. The history is critical for a correct diagnosis.

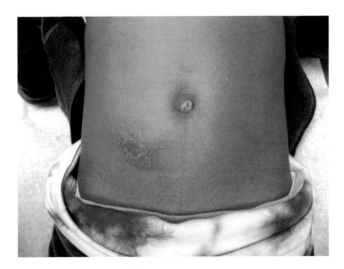

Figure 5.28 Herald patch of pityriasis rubra resembling a small burn on the lower abdomen of this 8-year-old African-American female.

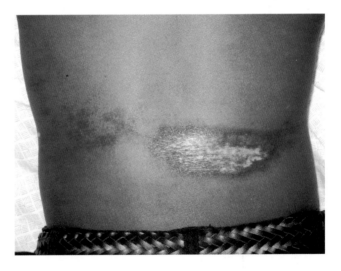

Figure 5.29 Morphea mimicking a large healed burn scar on this 8-year-old African-American female's lower abdomen.

Morphea

Morphea, the great imitator, can mimic large burn scars (Figure 5.29).

Pityriasis Rubra Pilaris

This disease typically spreads in a craniocaudal direction, beginning with redness and scales on the face and spreading downward on the body. Involvement of the palms of the hands and soles of the feet is almost invariable. The process may spread to the entire body[33] (Figure 5.30).

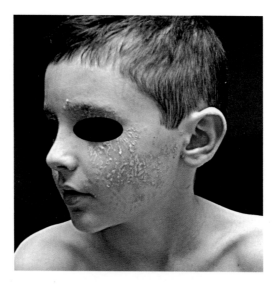

Figure 5.30 Pityriaris rubra pilaris began on the face of this young boy and will spread to the feet fairly rapidly. At this time the facial lesion resembles a mild burn with peeling.

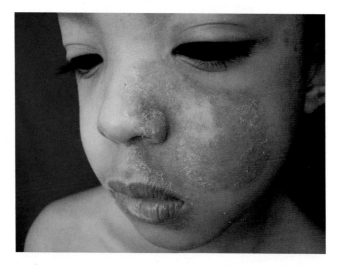

Figure 5.31 Longstanding untreated ringworm on almost half the face of this 5-year-old suggests the possibility of a caustic or thermal burn.

Ringworm/Tinea

These superficial fungus infections are well known, commonplace, contagious, and ordinarily easily recognized. Longstanding large untreated or recurrent lesions can be confusing (Figure 5.31).

Seborrheic Dermatitis

Large circular scaly areas of seborrheic dermatitis can mimic healing burns. However, the lesion will be found to be asymptomatic and the child to be well. Seborrheic dermatitis characteristically presents as a red scaling eruption that is nonpruritic and mild. The location on the cheek of this child is a bit unusual (Figure 5.32). The scalp, neck, trunk, and intertrigenous areas of the extremities are the most likely sites.[34]

Staphylococcal Scalded Skin Syndrome

As stated earlier in this chapter, SSSS is most often confused with a burn (Figure 5.33; compare with Figure 5.20).

Epidermolysis Bullosa (Blistering Diaper Dermatitis)

Epidermolysis bullosa is an inherited connective tissue disorder in which defects in keratin and collagen genes produce extremely fragile skin with separation and blistering between

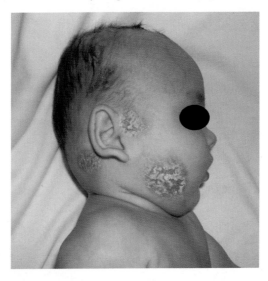

Figure 5.32 Seborrheic dermatitis in a somewhat unusual location on this infant's cheek. Redness and central scaling mimic a healing, peeling burn.

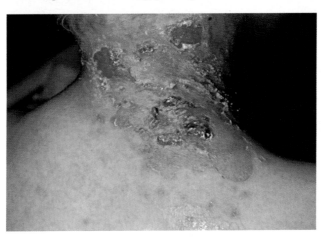

Figure 5.33 Staphylococcal scalded skin syndrome lesion on the neck and shoulder of this young boy resembles a rather extensive healing burn, perhaps a scalding injury with peripheral splash marks.

the epidermis and dermis. It primarily affects infants and young children. Minor trauma (i.e., rubbing, scratching, friction from diapers or clothing, removal of adhesives) can precipitate blistering and separation. There is no cure. Treatment is supportive.[35] There is some evidence of increased incidence in Arabic population groups[36] (Figure 5.34).

Junctional Epidermolysis Bullosa

Junctional epidermolysis bullosa is a severe subtype of the above entity. Here the bullous separation takes place at the deepest layer within the basement membrane of the

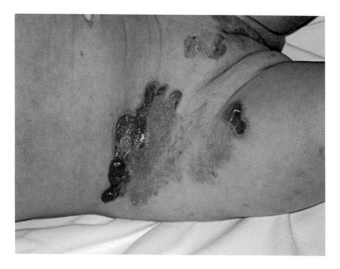

Figure 5.34 Epidermolysis bullosa in the genital area and groin of an infant female. The appearance simulates an accidental scalding burn trapped in a diaper fold, or an intentional scalding.

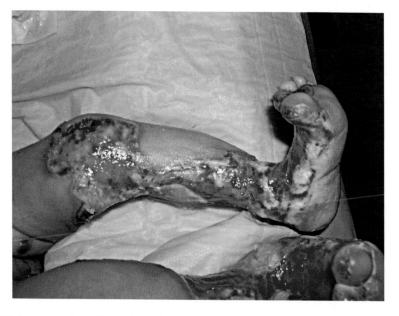

Figure 5.35 Junctional epidermolysis bullosa in an infant could be mistaken for a terrible immersion burn of both lower extremities.

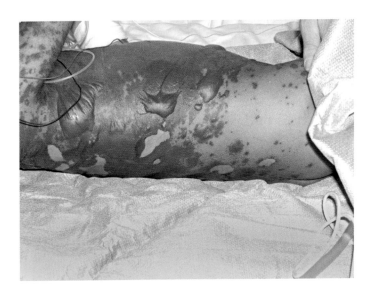

Figure 5.36 Toxic epidermal necrolysis. Sheet-like separation of skin and mucosa over the entire body. Differentiation from a massive burn requires careful investigation. (Reproduced from Palusci, V.J., and Fischer, H., *Child Abuse and Neglect: A Diagnostic Guide*, Manson Publishing Ltd., London, UK, with permission.)

integument[36] (Figure 5.35), mimicking a massive immersion burn to both lower extremities of a 6-week-old African-American baby (Figure 5.35).

Toxic Epidermal Necrolysis (Steven Johnson Syndrome)

Toxic epidermal necrolysis is a dreadful, acute, potentially fatal reaction to medication causing sheet-like separation of the outer layer of skin and mucosa all over the body. Literally hundreds of medications and some vaccines have been associated with its onset. Optimal treatment is best obtained in a hospital-based dedicated burn unit[37] (Figure 5.36).

References

1. Lane, W.G. 2003. Diagnosis and management of physical abuse in children. *Clin Fam Pract* 5:493–514.
2. Wheeler, D.M., and Hobbs, C.J. 1988. Mistakes in diagnosing non-accidental injury: 10 years experience. *Br Med J* 286:1233–36.
3. Stewart, G.M., and Rosenberg, N.M. 1996. Conditions mistaken for child abuse: Part II. *Pediatr Emerg Care* 12:217–21.
4. Pressel, D.M. 2000. Evaluation of physical abuse in children. *Am Fam Physician* 61:3057–64.
5. Kirschner, R.H., and Stein, R.J. 1985. The mistaken diagnosis of child abuse: A form of medical abuse? *Am J Dis Child* 139:873–75.
6. Wardinsky, T.D., and Vizcarrondo, F.E. 1995. The mistaken diagnosis of child abuse: A three-year USAF Medical Center analysis and literature review. *Military Med* 160:15–20.
7. Weinberg, S., Prose, N.S., and Shapiro, L. 1990. *Color atlas of dermatology*, 2nd ed. McGraw-Hill, New York, 137, 216.
8. Zitelli, B.J., and Davis, H.W. 2007. *Atlas of pediatric physical diagnosis*, 5th ed. Mosby/Elsevier, Philadelphia, 204.

9. Brown, J., and Melinkovich, P. 1986. Schönlein-Henoch pupura mis-diagnosed as suspected child abuse: A case report and literature review. *JAMA* 2256:617–18.
10. Zitelli, B.J., and Davis, H.W. 2007. *Atlas of pediatric physical diagnosis*, 5th ed. Mosby/Elsevier, Philadelphia, 302–3.
11. Weinberg, S., Prose, N.S., and Shapiro, L. 1990. *Color atlas of dermatology*, 2nd ed. McGraw-Hill, New York, 187.
12. Petersen, L.S., Nelson, A.M., Su, W.P., Mason, T., O'Fallon, W.M., and Gabriel, S.E. 1997. The epidemiology of morphia (localized scleroderma) in Olmstead Co. 1960–1993. *J Rheumatol* 24:73–80.
13. Petersen, L.E., Nelson, A.M., and Su, W.P. 1995. Classification of morphea (localized scleroderma). *Mayo Clin Proc* 70:1068–76.
14. Emery, H. 1998. Pediatric scleroderma. *Semin Cutan Med Surg* 17:41–47.
15. Zitelli, B.J., and Davis, H.W. 2007. *Atlas of pediatric physical diagnosis*, 5th ed. Mosby/Elsevier, Philadelphia, 258–60.
16. Weinberg, S., Prose, N.S., and Shapiro, L. 1990. *Color atlas of dermatology*, 2nd ed. McGraw-Hill, New York, 166–67.
17. Zitelli, B.J., and Davis, H.W. 2007. *Atlas of pediatric physical diagnosis*, 5th ed. Mosby/Elsevier, Philadelphia, 304.
18. Meneghini, C.L., and Bonifazi, E. 1986. *An atlas of pediatric dermatology*. Yearbook, Chicago, 58.
19. Graham, J.A., Hansen, K.K., Rabinowitz, L.G., and Esterly, N.B. 1994. Pyoderma gangrenosum in infants and children. *Pediatr Dermatol* 11:10–17.
20. Loening-Baucke, V. 1991. Lichen sclerosis et atrophicus in children. *Am J Dis Child* 145:1058–61.
21. Rushto, D.I. 1983. Amniotic band syndrome. *Br Med J* 286:919–20.
22. Walter, J.H., Jr., and Goss, L.R. 1998. Amniotic band syndrome. *J Foot Ankle Surg* 37:325–32.
23. Cohen, H.A., Matalon, A., Mezer, A., et al. 1997. Striae in adolescents mistaken for physical abuse. *J Fam Pract* 45:84–85.
24. Ossoff, R., and Giunta, J.L. 1978. The staphylococcal scalded skin syndrome versus erythema multiforms. *Oral Surg Oral Med Oral Pathol* 40:126–29.
25. Patel, G.K., and Finlay, A.Y. Staphylococcal scaled skin syndrome: Diagnosis and management. *Am J Clin Dermatol* 2003; 4:165–75.
26. Meneghini, C.L., and Bonifazi, E. 1986. *An atlas of pediatric dermatology*. Yearbook, Chicago, 138–41.
27. Wells, C.C., and Smith, N.V. 1979. Eosinophilic cellulitis. *Br Dermatol* 100:101–9.
28. Fenniche, S., Triki, S., Benmousley, R., Marrak, H., Ben Ammar, F., and Mokhtar, I. 2005. Lupus erythematosis in children: A report of six cases. *Dermatol Online J* 11(2):11.
29. Weinberg S., Prose N.S., and Shapiro L. 1990. *Color atlas of dermatology*, 2nd ed. McGraw-Hill, New York, 135.
30. Still, J.S., and Moyer, D.G. 1966. Schamberg's disease. *Arch Dermatol* 94:626–27.
31. Bowers, S., and Warshaw, E.M. 2006. Pityriasis licenoides and its subtypes. *J Am Acad Dermatol* 55:557–72.
32. Zitelli, B.J., and Davis, H.W. 2007. *Atlas of pediatric physical diagnosis*, 5th ed. Mosby/Elsevier, Philadelphia, 315–16.
33. Griffin, W.A. 1980. Pityriatic rubra pilaris. *Clin Exp Dermatol* 5:105–12.
34. Zitelli, B.J., and Davis, H.W. 2007. *Atlas of pediatric physical diagnosis*, 5th ed. Mosby/Elsevier, Philadelphia, 285.
35. Fine, J.-D. 2010. Inherited epidermolysis bullosa. *Orphanet J Rare Dis* 5:12.
36. Nakano, A., Lastringont, G.G., Paperna, T., et al. 2002. Junctional epidermolysis bullosa in the Middle East: Clinical and genetic studies in a series of cosanguinous families. *J Acad Dermatol* 46:510–16.
37. Pereira, F.P., Mudgil, A.V., Rossman, D.M., et al. 2007. Toxic epidermal necrolysis. *J Am Acad Dermatol* 56:181–200.

Afterword

The concept of intentional abuse of infants and children has been accepted for more than half a century. Its physical manifestations have been intensively described and promulgated throughout the civilized world. Yet the diagnosis of physical abuse of children is complex, not simple. The signs of accidental and nonaccidental injury can be indistinguishably identical. As exemplified in the preceding pages, the diagnostic challenge is confused further by a host of nontraumatic conditions imitating physical injury.

Many factors peripheral to the actual or purported incident and its etiology must enter into the equation of causality. We have referred to them as context.

Laws mandate reportage of suspicion of child abuse without fear of repercussions if that supposition is found to be in error. This lawful duty lays a heavy burden on persons of varied experience, education, or training whose activity or occupation places them in contact with children. Consequently, a decision for or against abuse may be equivocal or indeterminate, rather than clear-cut.

The law leans always in favor of the child, as it should, when uncertainty exists. This tends to encourage overzealousness. Certainly, we do not advocate endangering a child by delayed reporting. Neither would we urge a rush to judgment. We would strongly encourage consultation for a second opinion when in doubt. If at all possible, rely on someone with expertise in a medical specialty appropriate to the case—radiologists, dermatologists, pediatricians, ER physicians, pathologists, or any other "expert"—especially those who have *extensive experience with infants and children.*

Children Are Not Little Adults

Index